T0341211

Routledge Revivals

Industrial Relations in the Common Market

Originally published in 1972, *Industrial Relations in the Common Market* is a comparative study of the members of the Common Market, exploring the range of industrial relations and some of the contemporary issues and problems that they faced.

The book provides a comprehensive description of the Common Market, its economic growth and the diverse economies of the member countries. It also examines political parties and trade unions, and deals with the themes of collective bargaining, incomes policy, law and labour relations, industrial democracy, labour mobility and social security.

Industrial Relations in the Common Market is an excellent insight into the history of industrial relations within this economic community.

Industrial Relations in the Common Market

By Campbell Balfour

Routledge
Taylor & Francis Group

First published in 1972
by Routledge & Kegan Paul Ltd.

This edition first published in 2020 by Routledge
2 Park Square, Milton Park, Abingdon, Oxon, OX14 4RN
and by Routledge
605 Third Avenue, New York, NY 10017

Routledge is an imprint of the Taylor & Francis Group, an informa business

© Campbell Balfour 1972

Publisher's Note
The publisher has gone to great lengths to ensure the quality of this reprint but points out that some imperfections in the original copies may be apparent.

Disclaimer
The publisher has made every effort to trace copyright holders and welcomes correspondence from those they have been unable to contact.

A Library of Congress record exists under LCCN: 72090115

ISBN 13: 978-0-367-62111-7 (hbk)
ISBN 13: 978-1-003-10799-6 (ebk)

Industrial relations in the Common Market

By the same author
Incomes Policy and the Public Sector

INDUSTRIAL RELATIONS IN THE COMMON MARKET

Campbell Balfour

Department of Industrial Relations,
University College, Cardiff

Routledge & Kegan Paul
London and Boston

First published 1972
by Routledge & Kegan Paul Ltd
Broadway House, 68–74 Carter Lane,
London EC4V 5EL and
9 Park Street,
Boston, Mass., 02108, U.S.A.

ISBN 0 7100 7436 0 (c)
7437 9 (p)

For Lesley and Wendy

Contents

Preface

The Common Market is on the brink of an expansion of member countries, from the original six to ten. It will be the largest economic unit in the world, with 250 million people, greater than the USA or the USSR. In spite of its size, and its fifteen years of activity, comparatively little is known in Britain about important areas of the Market, to which the country (or parliament) has committed itself.

One of these areas is industrial relations. While a small number of studies exist of different West European countries, they are usually written by a group of authors, each dealing with a separate country, and sometimes using a different framework of analysis.

Now that the British government and people have entered the Common Market, there is a need for an introductory study of industrial relations in member countries: France, Germany, Italy, Belgium, Luxembourg, Holland, and the entrants Denmark, Norway and Ireland, who now join Britain.

As this study covers a large number of countries, many areas have had to be dealt with briefly. My intention has been to show the range of industrial relations, some of the current issues and problems in these countries, and to point out various sources and books which will take the curious further into the chosen area. The layout of this book is not separate country studies but comparative. as the studies are horizontal following particular subjects country by country.

At the same time, while there are a number of quoted studies available in English, much of the research on various aspects of industrial relations can only be done in the language of the particular country. Specialists in British industrial relations do not appear to be linguists, as there is little research done in Europe, though this may be due more to lack of money than to the linguistic modesty of the English.

My own experience of Europe amounted to two years in Italy and two years in Germany, with some months in France, so that I can cope at least with the reading of these three languages. While this is no substitute for living and working in western Europe, I hope this survey will encourage people to read about industrial relations in at least the major languages of western Europe, to travel and work there, and almost certainly, to help produce what will be a growing literature in the development of an expanding European Community.

My research has been assisted by the information sent by the London embassies of the member countries of the EEC and by the entrant countries. The office of the European Community in London has sent many pamphlets and fact sheets.

My knowledge of Norwegian industrial relations was greatly helped by Jon Ivarson, Harry Hanson, Lars Bjorheim and Nils Schjander, with whom I travelled through Asia as an ILO/NORAD team in 1971.

Lastly, there are the numerous scholars whose work has been acknowledged in the following pages. In a wide-ranging study of this type some mistakes may occur, in spite of numerous checks and enquiries. The omission of historical developments in the different countries was inevitable in a short work of this kind. Any errors or misinterpretations are due to, as Dr Johnson once said to the lady who asked him why his Dictionary defined a fetlock wrongly, 'Ignorance, Madam. Simple Ignorance.'

Abbreviations

Trade unions

CFDT	Confédération Française Démocratique du Travail
CGIL	Confederazione Generale Italiana del Lavoro
CGT	Confédération Générale du Travail
CGT—FO	Confédération Générale du Travail—Force Ouvière
CISC	Confédération Internationale des Syndicats Chrétiens
CISL	Confederazione Italiana Sindicati Lavoratori
CNV	Christelijk Nationaal Vakverbond in Nederland
CSC	Confédération des Syndicats Chrétiens
CGD	Christlicher Gewerkschaftsbund Deutschlands
FGTB	Fédération Générale du Travail du Belgique
KAB	Nederlandse Katholieke Arbeidebewegung
NVV	Nederlands Verbond van Vakverenigingen
TUC	Trades Union Congress
UIL	Unione Italiana del Lavoro
WCL	World Confederation of Labour
WFTU	World Federation of Trade Unions (Communist)
ICFTU	International Confederation of Free Trade Unions

Other organisations

ECSC	European Coal and Steel Community
EEC	European Economic Community
EFTA	European Free Trade Association
ILO	International Labour Organisation
OECD	Organisation for Economic Co-operation and Development
OEEC	Organisation for European Economic Co-operation

Introduction : Industrial relations in Britain

As this book has been written primarily for British readers, who have access to much of the literature of British industrial relations, Britain has not been included in the text, except by comparison, with the other Common Market countries. However, this short sketch is included as a checkpoint for those who wish a point of reference with the countries mentioned, as well as for those readers overseas who do not know the British system well.

The economy

Britain has had a slow growth rate since the end of World War II, with just over 2 per cent per annum, the lowest in western Europe, along with a chronic balance of payments problem, which affected and was in turn influenced by, the fact that sterling was a world currency. For a variety of reasons, the slow growth rate has been attributed to a general lack of purpose and efficiency in industry, the reluctance to introduce new methods and machinery, evidenced by the low rate of capital investment, probably the lowest in western Europe, on the part of management, and the reluctance to change and the general obstructionist attitude on the part of labour. There is a considerable literature on this, though some of it is a reflection of the latent masochism of the British directed towards themselves.

Trade unions and politics

The system of government is based on the two-party system, government and opposition, with the present Conservative government alternating with the Labour Party, which was in power from 1964 to 1970. The third parliamentary party, the Liberal, is small

1

and has little effect on parliament, though perhaps more in certain types of influence and ideas. The Conservatives have been the dominant party in Britain, which means in practice that they have had the vote, from time to time, of relatively large numbers of the working class. The Labour Party, in some seventy years of existence, has been in full power for only two six-year periods since 1945 (1945–51 and 1964–70). The trade union movement is officially and overwhelmingly affiliated to the Labour Party, and gives it its financial sinews. The Trade Union Congress's effect on policy varies with the nature of the government. Both Conservative and Labour governments usually consult with the trade unions, with the Labour government paying more attention to the views expressed. Modern society has meant that both parties have had to take attitudes to, or pass legislation about, industrial disputes and cost-push inflation. The Labour government brought in an incomes policy with union support which later crumbled, and legislation about industrial disputes which they later withdrew. The Conservatives consulted less than Labour, brought in a negative incomes policy designed to reduce wage increases in the public sector, and reinforced this by an unemployment level of over one million (4 per cent), and an Industrial Relations Act which was the first major change in trade union law for 100 years.

Union structure There are over 500 unions with a total membership of some 10,000,000, most of whom are affiliated to the TUC. Unions are based on the principles of craft, industrial and general unionism, with the Transport and General Workers being the largest with 1½ million members. The former craft union, the Engineers, has now developed into a multi-industrial union with over one million members. There are other large unions, although the Miners and Railwaymen have now slipped in size behind the Teachers and the Local Government Officers, reflecting the changing patterns of an industrial society. Frequent demands for more industrial unions, or more mergers between unions, have been made for years by critics inside and outside the trade union movement. Some mergers have taken place, e.g. Engineers with Foundry Workers and with Vehicle Builders. But the process has been slow.

Collective bargaining

The collective bargaining system in Britain is difficult to describe, as it covers the multiplicity of unions and structures described above. In the past, much of the bargaining has been on a national level, with minimum rates and conditions being agreed and used as a base in various regions and industries. The Donovan Report said that there had been a shift away from national bargaining to more local negotiations; and used the engineering industry as one of its examples. This trend has taken place and is partly due to the inflationary situation since the War, the shortage of labour and the rise of more powerful shop steward committees who are able to negotiate better and speedier earnings and conditions than the traditional national bargaining would have done. However, there are numbers of important negotiations still conducted at national level, notably in the large and growing public service sector.

Until recently the characteristic feature of the British system has been its voluntarism, the verbal or 'gentleman's agreement' between employer and union being the basis for much negotiation. The absence of contractual relations has been seen as a virtue rather than a defect, and it was only rarely that lawyers were called to assist.

The trends referred to above, the inflationary spiral, high labour demand and high money wages, leading in the late 1960s to more shop steward power and more unofficial strikes, led to a rising demand for more law and consequently, it was hoped, more stability in industrial relations.

Incomes policy

Attempts were made to stabilise prices and wages by voluntary agreement or exhortation by various Chancellors who, except for the 1948 attempt by a Labour government, were largely unsuccessful. In 1964, the Labour Party returned to power after thirteen years, pledged to introduce an incomes policy. A declaration of intent was signed between the CBI and the TUC agreeing to co-operate in economic growth, stable prices and moderate wage demands. A National Board for Prices and Incomes was set up as an independent body to interpret government policy, and to bring analysis and judgment to wage claims which were referred to it by the Secretary of State for Labour.

The policy did not succeed in containing inflation, as there were numerous financial crises which forced the government to introduce a credit 'squeeze' and damp down demand and growth. A weak balance of payments was a constant threat to sterling. After an incomes and prices standstill, earnings continued to rise at about 8 per cent per annum, against a growth rate of 2 per cent. Devaluation came in November 1967, which helped trade but led to an eventual rise in prices and costs. By 1969 earnings were rising more rapidly and by 1970, which was the year of the general election, rates were rising at 14 per cent, and the cost of living by 10 per cent.

The new Conservative government came to power pledged to end controls on wages and prices. Inflation continued and they introduced a negative incomes policy 'N−1', with each settlement in the public sector being at a lower level than the preceding one. This worked for some months, then exploded with the miners' strike, and the government, through a Court of Inquiry, had to settle at nearly 30 per cent. The collapse of the positive incomes policy of the Labour government and the negative one of the Conservative government, in spite of a million unemployed, had led to action on the field of trade union law.

Labour and the law
Industrial relations had functioned, unlike most Continental countries, almost without law. The main Acts had been those of 1871 and 1875, amended in 1906. Trade unions could not be sued in tort, although individual members could be charged with breaches of the law, e.g. for assault or damages, as any other citizen could be. The chief motive for the reform of the law appeared to be the growing number of unofficial strikes. In the late 1960s nearly 95 per cent of all strikes were unofficial, without the sanction or approval of the union official leadership, although in a number of cases the strike was later sanctioned. The pattern of strikes was short and frequent, and used as an effective bargaining weapon against firms with large export orders or a booming home market, such as the car industry. The pattern changed after 1970 and strikes became long-term and official.

The Industrial Relations Act 1971

This had been preceded by several years of discussion and argument. The Royal Commission on Trade Unions and Employers Associations (Donovan Report) had sat from 1965 to 1968 and produced a Report largely supporting the system of voluntarism, although recommending an improvement in procedures and contracts over a period, after which it might be possible to make contracts enforceable at law by agreement. The Labour government attempted to bring in reforms designed to inhibit unofficial strikes through fines and by setting up a Commission of Industrial Relations, to provide legislation on unfair dismissals, to register collective agreements and to review trade union rules. Union pressures and the reactions of the trade union MPs forced them to drop the legislation.

The Conservative government introduced similar but more far-reaching measures in the Industrial Relations Act of 1971, whose main measures came into force on 28 February 1972. The Act, which was bitterly opposed by the Labour Party and the trade unions, set out to provide a legal framework for industrial relations; there was the right to join, or not to join, a union; the right to form a union; protection against unfair dismissal; a legal obligation to register in order to come under the Act (though this was sidestepped by the unions in a gesture of non-compliance rather than defiance); definition of 'unfair' practices for both employers and labour; the creation of a National Commission on Industrial Relations, with greater powers than that visualised under the Labour Party proposal; a 'cooling-off' period for national or strategic strikes, a balloting of members before strikes, and other legislation known to other countries but new to Britain. The trade unions said that they would not co-operate, either by registration or by appearing before the expanded system of industrial tribunals. The National Industrial Relations Court (NIRC) is an example of a labour court, European style. NIRC had made a great impact on British industrial relations by mid-1972. The transport workers were fined £55,000 for contempt of court (non-appearance, and for failing to control the actions of their docker members). NIRC's ruling that shop stewards were agents of the union, and that the union was liable for their breaching or defying the court order, may have far-reaching effects. But the Act will only work effectively where there is co-operation by unions and their members. This lies yet in the future, although TUC policy has changed on a few points, e.g. unions may now defend themselves before the NIRC. The TUC decision not to register under the Act and to refuse nomination to the NIRC or the Industrial Tribunals still stands in 1972.

Strikes

In the 1950s and early 1960s, British industry was not particularly strike prone, except for one or two sectors, such as mining. Then the number of stoppages began to increase, until the short, sharp unofficial strike became the characteristic mark of the increasing power of shop stewards and the inflationary spiral. After 1970 the number of stoppages began to decline but the number of man days lost per worker increased. This marked the new trend towards the official and lengthy strike such as the postal workers in 1971 and the miners in 1972. The striking increase in days lost can be seen from the figures.

	No. of disputes	Working days lost (in thousands)
1967	2,116	2,787
1968	2,378	4,690
1969	3,116	6,846
1970	3,906	10,890
1971	2,223	13,558

(Department of Employment Gazette, Dec. 1971, Jan. 1972)

It has been argued that the short unofficial strike is more damaging to industry, as many managers pay and raise prices rather than lose markets and customers. The Industrial Relations Act of 1971 set out to discourage the unofficial strike by legal and other sanctions, but its effect will not be seen for some years. The Donovan Report and the TUC have argued that stronger trade unions can exercise more effective control over members than the law can, providing that contracts and procedures in negotiations are improved.

Industrial democracy

Britain, like a number of other countries, brought in some works committees and joint industrial councils after 1919, as a result of the Whitley Committee of 1917, and the Industrial Courts Acts of 1919. Most of the committees then formed did not last long, though some provided a link of consultation until World War II, when a number of Joint Production Committees were formed to help the war effort and channel the co-operation of the workers. Most of these vanished after the end of the war.

The main political impetus for their revival came from the Labour Party and the TUC, who both issued programmes supporting workers' participation in the post-war nationalisation of some industries, particularly in the coal industry. Consultation was made statutory in the nationalised industries, through the various Acts of parliament, and consultative committees were established at different levels, from local to national. The post-war Labour government tried to revive the joint consultation methods of wartime, and these did take some root in a number of firms, though not to the extent hoped for.

Joint consultation failed to transform the militant miners into co-operative workers and their strike rate rose through the 1950s. Other nationalised industries did not have great success with consultation, although the electricity supply industry appeared to have a good record of industrial relations. Significantly, electricity supply was a more prosperous industry than mining, and a number of effective consultative committees have flourished in some of the larger and more prosperous firms.

There was a revival of interest in industrial democracy in the 1960s, partly as a militant left-wing leadership came into power in some unions who recognised the growing power of shop stewards and saw an opportunity to create 'democracy on the shop floor'. The Labour Party to appear to have revived a continuing interest in the subject, although their main creation as a government in the 1960s was the development of the experiment of worker directors in the recently nationalised steel industry. The Report of March 1972 on the performance of worker directors in steel posed the problem of relating the workers at plant level with their twelve representatives at board level.

Social security

The chief point of difference between the British system and that of the Common Market countries is that the British National Health Service is fully comprehensive, whereas in several other countries on the Continent the patient pays the doctor then claims the money from insurance funds (France, Belgium, Luxembourg) and in others the doctor is paid by the insurance fund while the patient pays some part of the cost (Germany, Italy and Holland).

Another point of difference is the method of financing social security. The British scheme is financed mainly through direct taxation on the whole working population, while in the Common Market countries, the state pays a smaller amount and the employer and the worker pay correspondingly more.

The most controversial aspects of the relation between social security and industrial relations in recent years has been the high degree of absenteeism in industry. Some observers argue that much sickness is 'phoney' and calculations of work days lost run into the hundred thousand or quarter million yearly mark. Related to this has been the growing practice of strikers to draw social security for their families, as they are entitled to by law. They were also able to claim income tax rebate, and this added up to a minimum standard of living during a strike. Legislation in 1971 reduced this somewhat, but it was estimated during the 1972 miners' strike that the 250,000 official strikers drew some £1 million weekly for several weeks, or their families did. The Mineworkers' Union paid no strike pay, and some critics argued that this could represent a new form of strike tactic in that strikes could be financed from social security. This may lead to further changes in the system of giving social benefits to strikers' families, but the counter arguments, based on the humanitarian principle, are strong.

The effects of the Common Market on industrial relations

The aspirations and objectives of the Treaty of Rome are super-imposed on a variety of countries and institutions, with different history and culture. Some people hold the view that the various member countries, and those who are now joining (Denmark, Norway, Ireland and Britain) will be poured into a giant cooking pot and remoulded into a new shape by the kitchens of the EEC.

This may happen in time, but it is so far away from reality that we restrict ourselves to looking at what is happening in the Community now with the original six countries, what is happening in the four who are joining, then we speculate on the possible implications of membership in the next decade or so.

The benefits for industry seem to be agreed by industrialists, with some reservations from those whose firms are exposed to a new competition, and the growth rate of the Common Market countries has been considerably in advance of that of the UK. Disagreement exists as to whether the dynamic phase of west European expansion has died down, but there is little doubt that the productivity per head and the resulting standard of living is rising faster than in Britain, whichever period one chooses in the past fifteen years. Every country in the Six had a faster rise in hourly gross wages and a faster rise in real wages, with the rise in the latter being 65 per cent for the Six as compared with 20 per cent for the UK, over the period 1958-68.

This rapid rise in living standards explains why the trade unions of the Six, after some initial hesitation from some federations, wholeheartedly support the principle of the Common Market. They saw that a larger market would make for technical progress and that the resulting technological redundancy could be better fought by pooling resources in the EEC Social Fund, which would then be

9

channelled to the high unemployment areas such as southern Italy, and also to the areas faced with structural unemployment such as the coal and steel industries.

Ludwig Rosenberg, retiring president of the German DGB (the equivalent of the British TUC) said in London in 1971, 'There is no doubt in my mind that our aims of securing full employment, job security and improved working conditions ... the exclusion of unfair labour practices by national competition and all that—these tasks of trade unionism cannot be fulfilled satisfactorily as long as the present balkanisation of free and democratic Europe remains as it is' (quoted in *Trade Union News No. 5*, 1971, p. 11). Saying this, he spoke for the trade union movement of the Six with over 15 million members.

The effect on British industrial relations

Comments on the probable effects of British entry range from the Hallelujah to the Doomsday schools of politicians. The euphoric believe, as they hold the Common Market to be an economic crusade, that the British growth rate will rise sharply as British industry reacts with vigour to the 'cold bath' of competition. Managerial sloth and trade union bloody-mindedness will both disappear in the new industrial climate. The Doomsday school believe that industry will suffer from unrestricted competition, that we are too far from the 'golden triangle' of the Ruhr and northern France, and that Britain will become the 'Northern Ireland' of the Common Market, with high unemployment and periodical devaluations.

As usual, the truth lies somewhere between the two extremes. Industry will be exposed to greater competition, once the cosy tariff walls around Britain are breached by the Treaty and a free market is created for over 200 million people. Industry will have to raise its productivity and improve efficiency. The methods of raising productivity and efficiency have been known to British industry for over twenty years (see the *Anglo-American Productivity Reports*, British Productivity Council, London, 1948–53) but it has been largely unsuccessful in implementing them. Whether management or men are mostly to blame for this state of affairs is now water under the bridge. The need for greater output may help to change the present climate of industrial relations, providing that the mere act of joining the Market is not regarded as a magic ointment which will heal minds and tongues.

We cannot turn and point to any industrial relations system among the Six and say, 'We will follow that example and cure ourselves', for each has its strong and weak points. We should also remember that the German system, with its low strike figures and productive workers, may function because they are German, and not because of the system.

The systems of the Market countries (here we include the four also) vary widely and there is not even a Community norm of industrial relations. The German system rests on a small number of well-organised industrial unions and employers' associations, with a logical and disciplined legal framework for the collective bargaining which takes place. By contrast, the French system is sprawling and untidy, more voluntaristic than the German, and with a trade union movement which is divided three or four ways on religious or political grounds: the employers tend to be conservative and less receptive to unions than are the German employers; firms tend to be small and family dominated; collective bargaining is fragmented and buttressed by law on account of the weakness of the unions.

The Dutch system is closer to the German in its orderliness, but the trade unions are fragmented, as are those of the Belgians and the Italians. Their similarities and differences are described in the following chapters.

Harmonisation

There are two main ways by which Britain, and the other three entrants, will be influenced by the Common Market in the field of industrial relations. One is by the influence of competitive pressures and meetings, the devising of common policies by employers and, for their part, by trade unions. The new development of the multi-national firm, spanning western Europe and reaching back at times mainly into the United States and sometimes to Japan, is matched by the rise of multinational union activity, although this is still in the conference and policy discussion stage. This international *'jeu sans frontières'* has few spectators apart from other business competitors and the EEC Commission. The Commission stands for the principle of the Treaty of Rome, a market founded on the free movement of the factors of production, including capital. This principle runs against the facts of economic organisation, which show that in some industries larger firms achieve economies of scale and lower unit costs, raising their productivity and profitability. This leads to mergers of firms and charges of monopoly, which the Commission has to deplore. A *modus vivendi* is usually found.

The labour policies of the giant firms stand like a lighthouse on the industrial landscape and attract the attention of other unions. In this way, policies which began in a large firm and appeal to unions, eventually penetrate in various forms to other smaller firms, who fit the policies to their mode of production, technology and markets.

The other way by which countries are influenced is by the policy of harmonisation contained in the Treaty of Rome.

While this does not refer to industrial relations between member countries, some trends will soon be followed in Britain. One of these trends could be worker participation which gives employees an opportunity to discuss economic and social matters. The EEC are encouraging this development by legislation; they favour a development similar to that of co-determination in Germany with workers having one-third of the seats on the supervisory board. In four of the six countries in the Common Market, Germany (West Germany is referred to as Germany throughout), France, Belgium and Holland, works councils are laid down by law according to the number of employees. In Italy and Scandinavia they have arisen by negotiation. There are different methods of electing such committees, some favour the unions while others tend to be separate from them. Their powers vary in the economic sphere but they have much influence in social spheres. In nearly all countries management have to submit reports and provide at least the same information as for the shareholders. Britain has followed this trend in some respect by the Industrial Relations Act of 1971, which states that workers should receive information necessary for negotiations.

Certain parts of the Treaty of Rome indicate equal pay for women and the harmonisation of labour costs, which could mean a levelling up of wages towards the higher paid countries. But equal pay for women is unlikely to become a major issue for some years, as all the countries of the Ten have signed the ILO Convention supporting the principle, and enforcement is left to individual governments.

In fact there has not been a widespread narrowing of wage differentials between countries as a result of the Common Market. There are greater differences between regions in the same country than there are between the national averages. Wage levels seem to depend more on the nature and type of the industry, and the larger plants show certain similarities in pay structures and levels. Some changes may take place as some shipbuilding and ship-repairing industries are higher cost than others. (On this subject see A. D. Butler, 'Labour Costs in the Common Market', *Industrial Relations*, February 1967, pp. 166-83.)

Collective bargaining is an area in which the Six are more likely to follow British trends than the reverse. The shift in western Europe is from national bargaining in a number of countries, buttressed by legislation, to more local and plant bargaining, described in Britain by the Donovan Report as the two systems of industrial relations. There is also a long-established yearning on the part of the European unions for more inter-Community solidarity between unions in order to reinforce and strengthen wage claims. If French miners were on strike, German miners should not supply the missing coal, nor steel workers the missing steel.

This argument gains more force with the recent labour troubles in the British car industry, in 1971 and earlier. Car firms with multi-national connections are said to be ready to transfer operations to more strike-free countries and even to build plants outside the Common Market in the cheaper labour areas of southern Europe, such as Spain, Portugal, Greece and Turkey. The same comments have been made about investment in the shipbuilding industry, which has higher labour costs in the industrialised countries. But multi-industrial and multi-national union operations lie some distance in the future. Conferences are held, as in the case of the transport workers, but the diversity of union aims may keep unity apart for the present. The differing systems of labour law would also handicap some national unions as opposed to others.

The effect on industrial disputes

There are those who believe that membership of the EEC will

greatly reduce the number of days lost through strikes by workers. Such views are more often found in Britain, due to a common belief that the British system of industrial relations is akin to an anarchist's football match where the referee has no whistle. The belief is also due to an ignorance as to strike patterns in other countries, which show that in the decade 1961–70, Britain came fourth among the ten countries of the Community, and if France had counted the large-scale strikes of 1968, Britain would have been half way down, or up, the league table.

No common factor is to be found in the variety of strike figures in the Community, as the two top countries lose forty times as many days as the two most peaceful. Comparability is also difficult, due to the different types of unions and the impact which strikes make, e.g. the British pattern of small, short unofficial strikes may be more disruptive than the large-scale Italian ones.

The above description of strike figures shows that the member countries of the EEC have found no panacea for strikes. Nor have they found workable systems of labour law which imposes sanctions on the strikers, although this varies in effectiveness from country to country.

Harmonisation of social policy

Possible effects in the field of social security may lead to changes in the incidence of taxation. The EEC countries rely less on general taxation and more on employer and individual contributions. The percentage of social security benefits to GNP is also higher in the Community, and we would expect that harmonisation would lead to an increase in social security benefits. Yet the British social services compare reasonably well with the others, particularly in the area of the National Health Service.

Britain lags behind in the number of paid holidays enjoyed by its labour force, and with other countries having from seven to twenty or more days of paid holidays and public ones combined, it seems likely that Britain will move some way towards the Continental pattern, rather than the reverse.

Labour mobility is bound to increase, both in the numbers who move and in the geographical areas which are covered, although Britain will have some difficulties with the status of Commonwealth citizens. This means greater emphasis on social policies such as redundancy and retraining for new jobs. The European Social Fund, described later in these pages, is an important step in giving support and strength to systems of worker protection and job finding. Britain is well behind in the area of job retraining, and the government in February 1971 announced plans for increasing the numbers being retrained by fivefold.

The future of industrial relations?

Whatever the effects of Common Market entry may be, the system of industrial relations is bound to be influenced by the country joining a large European market, whether this develops as a 'Europe des parties' or, as the visionaries see it, a parliament of Europe and an eventual federation. If the first concept, the Europe of countries, is the more powerful one, then the forces of competition and inter-nation rivalry, as well as the co-operation of business and unions across the frontiers of the different countries, will have a powerful and pervasive influence. If the federal idea develops, then there may be more parliamentary legislation bringing about changes reinforcing or influencing those already taking place through market and political forces.

Whichever idea of the Common Market becomes influential, British industrial relations will never be the same, nor is the country likely to return to the pre-Donovan voluntaristic system. Collective bargaining is likely to be more formalised and the collective agreement is likely to be more wide reaching in its coverage, as will be the expectations of industrial peace (or at least the following of agreed procedures for resolving disputes) during the life of the agreement. We still have the opportunity to make our own changes in the British system before international pressures, or the winds of competition and change make them for us. To do this we have to know the outline of the industrial relations systems of the Community, and to remember that the problems of industrial countries, from inflation to the need to create wealth and distribute it fairly, are common to us all.

② The Common Market

The history and structure of the Common Market, or the European Economic Community (EEC) is sufficiently well known to need no more than a brief summary here in order to sketch out the framework in which industry, politics, and industrial relations (affected also by the first two factors) will develop. An attempt will be made to distinguish between facts about the Common Market, e.g. the posters in 1971 saying 'Get the facts about the Common Market', and what in reality are opinions or estimates although they may be presented as 'facts'.

The Common Market was set up in March 1957 with the signing of the Treaty of Rome, whose objective is to remove the barriers to trading between the member countries. The principle here is that the free flow of goods, capital, and labour will, based on the principle of competition, raise production and therefore living standards. This principle only applies inside the Community, as there is a common tariff barrier applied against the rest of the world, with certain exceptions and adjustments. This arrangement is known to economists as a 'customs union', but the EEC, or a member of its leading protagonists, intended to work towards greater co-operation between member states, towards greater economic, social and monetary union, a single joint parliament and a common currency. There is disagreement over the latter aims between the group who believe in closer union, and those who, like the late General de Gaulle, believed in a union of separate national states, or a 'Europe des patries'.

During these developments, the British had not stayed out of Europe. They recognised that western Europe had special problems of reconstruction after 1945, and some countries wished for economic union to raise living standards, while others were anxious to achieve a political union so that a third European war in the twentieth century would be less likely (Europe in this context means western Europe). Western European recovery was greatly aided by American money, based on the Marshall Plan. The Americans and the British also joined the European countries in the Council of Europe, in 1949, and the North Atlantic Treaty Organisation (NATO) was formed in the same year. The British also entered into the Western European Union, on which economic, political and defence questions were discussed from 1954 onwards.

Prior to the formation of the EEC, the European Coal and Steel Community was formed by France, Germany, Belgium, Luxembourg, Italy and the Netherlands, who later formed the Six of the EEC. The intention of the ECSC was to plan and develop the coal and steel industries of the Community inside a common market. A detailed code of rules was drawn up for this purpose and the results were that steel production rose by 25 per cent in three years. The beneficial results of the ECSC was a factor in the founding of the EEC five years later.

Outside the EEC, the other seven West European countries: Austria, Denmark, Norway, Portugal, Sweden, Switzerland and UK, founded the European Free Trade Association (EFTA), whose aim was to reduce the tariff barriers between these countries and eventually create a free trade area. Though this was to function until Britain entered the EEC, it was never so successful a trading bloc as was the EEC.

Britain's application to join the Common Market in the early sixties was refused mainly by the French veto. The second attempt in 1967, under a different government, was also refused. This soured British public opinion against the EEC, which had up to then been mainly in favour. The negotiations began again and in 1971, under the new Conservative government which replaced the preceding Labour government, the terms were accepted.

The terms on entry

Agriculture Britain agreed to the Common Agricultural Policy (CAP) of the Six, thereby giving preference to Community produce and phasing out purchases from the Commonwealth. The new policy was to be reached in six steps over five years. Britain's payments to the Community budget would be 'a maximum annual

contribution ... in the first five years amounting to 8·65 per cent
... in 1973 rising to 18·92 per cent ... in 1977' (Mr Rippon in
parliament, *The Times*, 25 June 1971). Mr Rippon told parliament
that this sum would be rather less than the earlier estimate of the
previous December as the 'mountain of butter' had rapidly dis-
appeared from the EEC stockpile and the overall cost of price
support had fallen. Parliamentary and other estimates said that the
first price increases under the new policy would be made in April
1973 and the last in December 1977. Over the five years the retail
price index might rise by an added 3 to 4 per cent (some estimates
went as high as a 5 per cent price rise). This would work out at one
per cent or less per year, depending on the movement of food and
other prices. Economists and MPs in favour of entry pointed out
that as food prices were rising at 10 per cent yearly, an extra one
per cent was marginal compared with the benefits of entry.

Commonwealth   This could have been the sticking point for some
MPs, on both the right and the left. There was concern over the
sugar producers of the West Indies, who were among the poorer
countries discussed. The Six promised that special care would be
shown, and the British took this to mean that sugar sales to
Britain from those countries would be maintained at their present
figure of 1.4 million metric tons.

The point of several questions in parliament to Mr Rippon was
whether the EEC agricultural policy would mean no large-scale
food imports from New Zealand after 1977. On this point Mr
Rippon was able to satisfy those who were anxious to be satisfied,
saying that an enlarged Community would be a large buyer of milk
products and that new arrangements might be made in the future.
'New Zealand, ... six years hence, would be guaranteed sales of
136,000 tons of butter and at least 15,000 tons of cheese. These
are minimum guarantees ... Taken altogether, this represents a
very satisfactory deal ... (Cheers) (ibid.). But M. Pompidou's
speech to cheese producers in the Auvergne on 26 June, outlining
their new opportunities as New Zealand cheese 'tends to disappear'
have been widely reported and resented by anti-marketeers (*The
Times*, 29 June 1971).

Industry   Although Britain asked for a three-year transition
period, so that all tariffs between the partners would disappear, the

Six were successful in negotiating the same period of years as for agriculture. There will be five successive 20 per cent cuts in industrial tariffs. It was expected that investment would be effective from the date of entry as the tariff-free years would lie a short distance ahead. Some exceptions were made for some raw materials which Britain had to import from outside Europe, ranging from aluminium to zinc.

Coal, steel and Euratom　Britain entered into the arrangements for the above three, signing the Euratom Treaty as well as the European Coal and Steel Community (ECSC) agreement. The latter move led to criticism from Mr Wilson.

Sterling　There appeared to be no definite arrangements on sterling except in 'agreement to agree' that it should be phased out as a world reserve currency. Mr Rippon was under fierce questioning and gave vague answers: 'My difficulty was that sterling is not really part of the negotiations except on harmonisation of capital movements.' Three points would have special attention: 'the need to maintain international monetary liquidity, the need to ensure that there is no undue balance of payments burden, and the need to protect the interests of existing sterling holders' (*The Times*, 25 June 1971).

CAP and entry costs

The politicians were also worried about the long-term payments which will be a burden on the British balance of payments and of the effect on food prices which will tend to raise wages and therefore costs. The public were hostile to the idea of giving up the cheaper imported food in favour of buying dearer food from the Continent. This attitude is summed up by an economist in *The Times*, 12 May 1971 (Dr Josling, 'In or Out—an inevitable rise in food prices') who said of the CAP, 'It is widely accepted by friend and foe of British membership that this policy is a wildly expensive extravagance which would impose a severe burden on the British economy.' Dr Josling disagreed with this view and suggested that statistical projection of the costs of UK beef and wheat prices over the next seven years would show them converging upwards to reach harmony with EEC prices. Though Dr Josling was critical of the CAP, saying that 'it is very expensive in relation to its achievements', his researches have been widely quoted and used by financial journalists in calculating new estimates of the cost of entry. These are usually listed as (1) Extra Import Cost plus Levies. (2) Payment of Customs Duties to Community. (3) Payment of 1 per cent of VAT (Value Added Tax) yield. (4) Receipts, levy retentions, etc. The White Paper of 1970 (*Britain and the European Communities: an economic assessment*, Cmnd 4829, HMSO, London, 1970) made an attempt to quantify the costs ranging from an unspecified lower figure up to a maximum of £870 million, which would have been crippling to the economy.

The new calculations are more optimistic and range up to some £400 million, at least half the previous year's estimate. The reasons for the lower estimates are that British farmers will be stimulated by the higher prices for food to produce more (thereby reducing the amount of food imports needed and also the EEC contribution); that the British consumer will react to higher prices by switching his preferences from dearer to cheaper, from beef to pork, and butter to margarine. Unaware as the British public are of the deeper issues of Europeanisation, they know about food prices and this is the major reason given (58 per cent in a BBC poll) for opposing British entry. (The BBC poll of 28 June 1971 showed: Strongly For 8 per cent, For 13 per cent, Don't Know 21 per cent, Against 20 per cent, Strongly Against 38 per cent.)

The 'Payment Cost' of entry would rise if Britain were to devalue again. This would mean an increase in food prices in terms of sterling, as the Community rules fix farm prices in terms of gold, although there is usually a transitional period. As the economy is in a period of stagnation, a reflation could take place through devaluation. Several of the leading newspapers have urged the government to reflate, but the difficulty is that a rise in consumption usually takes place in advance of production and this would lead to more imports and a balance of payments deficit. The last Labour government attempted to improve the balance of payments by large increases in taxation which restricted consumption. The balance of payments improved but the cure turned out to be worse than the disease as production stagnated, investment fell and prices rose rapidly (about 8 per cent due to wage increases of 10 per cent yearly in 1969–70, and higher world food prices. This situation placed the Conservative government in a dilemma. They won the

1970 election by promising to start economic growth again without controls on wages and, by reducing taxation and providing incentives, to 'cut the rise in prices at a stroke'. This phrase has been quoted against Mr Heath *ad nauseam,* as the estimate at the end of his first year of office, on 24 June 1971, was that food prices had increased by 10 per cent over the year. Production had increased very little over the year and a half, a fact which was mainly due to the sharp rise in unemployment to some 900,000 in the UK. This is some 30 per cent higher than the figure in the last two years of the Labour government, which was criticised by the Conservative opposition as being much too high. This in turn has led to numbers of firms going bankrupt, of which the best known are Rolls Royce and Upper Clyde Shipbuilders. The forecast from some quarters is a gloomy one, with predictions of still rising prices, yet higher unemployment rising to the million mark by January, and wage inflation continuing. The government deny this and claimed in the economic debate of 28 June 1971, that inflation was slowing down and that the economy would soon recover. But inflation continued through 1972.

Reasons for entry

The government's main reason for entry was stated simply: it 'believes that membership of the European Economic Community will enable Britain to achieve a higher standard of living'. They pointed out that the Six have done this through their union. There would be hazards in entering, economic growth would not be automatic, but we would be entering, as ten countries (along with Ireland, Norway and Denmark), the largest population grouping in the industrialised world with over 250 million people, larger than the USSR or the USA.

Industry would be able to expand as the market would be far larger, the amount of available investment would be greater, there would be economies of scale. The costs of entry amounted to several million pounds yearly but 'Given a minimum increase, by the end of five years our national income could be some £1,000 million a year higher'. Statistics from the Six showed that the increase in average income per worker in real terms between 1958 and 1969 was as follows: Italy 92 per cent, France 77, Netherlands 74, Germany 72, Belgium 52, while Britain's slow growth over this period had meant an increase of only 39 per cent.

The disadvantages would be some loss of trade with the Commonwealth and other countries, which trade had already been declining over the past ten or fifteen years with the formation of new trading arrangements and the development of infant industries in new countries trying to become more self-sufficient. Britain would also have to buy dearer food and pay levies through the Community budget.

Objections from the Labour opposition and from public opinion centred mainly, though not exclusively, on the higher cost of food due to the CAP, although the costs of entry were expected to be more than offset by economic growth, so that national income per head would rise. The relevance of this claim for the mass of workers is obvious, and no discussion of industrial relations would be valid unless the relations between labour, management, government and economic growth are discussed.

The springs of economic growth

There is a lack of unanimity over the causes of economic growth and more particularly, whether membership of the Common Market will produce what has been called the 'X-efficiency factor' and rejuvenate the British economy. The most thorough examination of economic growth in recent years has been E. F. Denison's *Why Growth Rates Differ* (Brookings Institution, 1967) and the various countries in the Common Market (the Ten) are examined by him, in this, and other studies. Denison estimates the growth rates of real national income in two periods, 1950–64 and 1955–64. This gives an idea of the effect of the Common Market on these countries (the Rome Treaty dates from 1957), in the later period (see Table 1).

It can be seen from the Table that Britain has lagged behind for almost the whole of the post-war period. At first it was thought that the west European countries' more rapid growth was due to the low base from which they started their post-war recovery after war and occupation. But this explanation ceases to be adequate after a number of years and we must search for causes.

Several writers take labour as their measure, and talk of labour input; this includes the size of the labour force, its composition, the hours worked and the educational background of workers. As Britain had a high level of employment for the period 1945–65,

Table 1 *Percentage growth rate of real national income*

Country	National income		Nat. income per person employed		Nat. income per capita	
	1950-64	1955-64	1950-64	1955-64	1950-64	1955-64
Germany	7·1	5·6	5·3	4·3	5·9	4·3
Italy	5·6	5·4	5·2	5·4	4·9	4·7
France	4·9	5·0	4·7	4·7	3·8	3·7
Netherlands	4·9	4·3	3·7	3·1	3·5	2·9
Norway	3·8	3·9	3·6	3·7	2·9	3·0
Denmark	3·6	4·8	2·7	3·5	2·9	4·1
Belgium	3·4	3·5	2·8	3·0	2·8	2·9
UK	2·6	2·8	2·0	2·3	2·2	2·1

Adapted from E. F. Denison, 'Economic Growth' in *Britain's Economic Prospects*, R. Caves (ed.), Allen & Unwin, London, 1968, p. 232.

there was little surplus labour. Immigration was not high, and the influx of coloured workers from the Commonwealth raised community tensions and led to the Immigration Act of 1962 which stopped what had been virtually free labour mobility from the Commonwealth (prevented earlier by distance and costs of transportation, then aided by cheap charter flights in the late 1950s). By comparison, West Germany had a large labour intake from the east European refugees, including several millions from East Germany, an inflow which virtually stopped after the Berlin wall was built in 1961. Britain's population growth is low compared with some other countries. and the number of women in the labour force is relatively high as a result of wartime work, so that there was no great reservoir of womanpower to be tapped. Curiously enough, the British probably work more hours per week and produce less per head for it, than in some other comparable countries. From 1955–62 hours worked fell by 4 per cent in the UK, but by greater amounts in Norway, Netherlands, Belgium, Italy, Denmark, Germany, with 6·6, 6·5, 5·9, 7·9, 8·6, 13·1, respectively (Denison, 'Economic Growth', p. 241).

Capital input is also important, as some studies of the relative difference in productivity per head between British and American workers have shown (roughly measured in the 1950s, US workers produced twice as much per head, but also had twice the amount of horsepower). Most countries cited above had a higher rate of capital investment than had Britain. Besides immigration of labour and population increase, some countries have a large inflow of labour into industry from the agricultural sector. As many small traditional farms are high cost, and as the rural birth rate is higher than the urban, many farms have too much labour, inefficiently used, so that there is a high degree of under-employment. The labour is more effectively used in industry and the output per head in the country thereby rises. This was the case in France and especially in Italy.

Attempts have been made to measure the contribution of other factors but these pose certain difficulties. What is the contribution of increased education, is it a social good or a productive resource? Certainly better educated workers are potentially more capable of exercising their skills and judgments and increasing productivity, but this depends on the use to which they are put, and whether their education can be channelled into production.

Doubts about Britain's economic growth in the Common Market

While the arguments about the much larger consumer market, the economies of scale, the availability of capital, have convinced the greater part of British industry and brought the endorsement of the Confederation of British Industries (CBI), there are some weighty economic arguments which throw doubts on the optimistic prospects for British growth after entry.

Many of these objections are examined in an article in the *National Economic Review*, the journal of the National Institute of Economic and Social Research (NIESR), entitled 'Another look at the Common Market' (No. 54, November 1970, pp. 29–43). This points out that the crucial question put by the White Paper is 'whether our GNP ... can be expected to grow more quickly'. If not, then the cost of membership could be burdensome. This is offset by the 'dynamic effects' of membership. The Institute points out that these 'dynamic effects' are matters of opinion, and examines the effects of membership on the Community.

The study shows that the formation of the EEC had a beneficial effect by encouraging US investment, but the authors are doubtful about the 'dynamic effect' of entry, and say that the acceptance of the high costs of entry measured against the expectation that production would rise even more 'represent a triumph of hope over experience'. They point out that the Six are not expanding as quickly in output as they did in their earlier years, and that their growth has been partly due to the scaling down of their own internal tariffs. Britain does not stand to gain in the same way: 'It is hard to see anything which suggests that the UK's performance would improve more rapidly inside than outside the Community.'

As most of the argument about entry is measured against the UK's present and past economic position, the NIESR says that other west European countries outside the Community are on the edge of achieving high growth rates. The article shows that some of the high growth rates achieved by some countries, quoted as evidence of the benefits of EEC membership, were mainly due to the dwindling of the agricultural sector and the movement of men and resources to the manufacturing and service sectors with a consequent rise in the productivity of the first sector as it used labour more effectively, and of the other two sectors as they gained labour and made more effective use of it. Increase in trade and economies of scale are also examined as possible benefits and discounted. The conclusion of a long and searching study is that there is little 'which suggests that the United Kingdom's performance would be improved more rapidly inside than outside the Community' (*ibid.*, p. 43).

None the less, the fact that the authors come out against any great boost for the British economy as a result of entry does not mean that British industry will not benefit, although they are unable to demonstrate effectively that it would be so. The reverse aspect of the case for entry is the question, 'What could we do if we stayed out?' and the possible projections for growth there are even less predictable.

While Britain has a small agricultural sector (which means a high payment under the CAP), this does not mean that there is no surplus of labour. Part of the reason for Italy's high growth rate was that it had large numbers of unemployed, mainly in southern Italy, and economic expansion has drawn heavily on those. Britain now has a million unemployed (January–June 1972) and these represent, however repugnant the description may be, a reservoir for expansion. And much of the labour, in distinction to that of southern Italy, is more skilled and better educated so that it is potentially more productive.

Finally, there is a large amount of British labour which is underemployed, as some dramatic increases in output per head have been the result of numbers of productivity bargains in the 1960s. One industrial consultant has even argued that British industry is overmanned by a factor of two, and that Britain could produce twice as much with the same labour force, or the present output with half the labour force. However exaggerated the statement may be, there is much other evidence that British industry is often overmanned.

③ Economic growth and the economies of member countries

The frontiers of industrial relations in the various countries are enfolded by the economic framework and performance of their respective countries. As Britain frequently complains that her poor economic performance is due to excessive demand, inflation, high wage costs, low productivity, inefficient management, and other fiscal, monetary and trading aspects of this, it is instructive to look at the other countries in, and entering, the Community, in order to see if 'the British Disease' is unique to the UK.

France

Economic growth in France has been due to a number of factors, most of which would have occurred without the birth of the Community, though this had an external stimulating effect. After 1957 there was an expansion in the labour force as the war in Algeria ended and the army came back to civilian life, followed by large numbers of *'pieds noirs'*, the French-Algerians, and the resulting release of resources to industry from military use. These resources were put to good use by the French system of planning. One writer thinks that the effects of the plans were not so much the physical planning and allocation of resources, but the changing of businessmen's attitudes 'basically changing the psychological outlook of business' (C. P. Kindleberger, *Europe's Postwar Growth*, Harvard University Press, Cambridge, Mass., 1967, p. 59). France had a large agricultural sector and many small businesses. A large part of the labour force was under-employed in inefficient industries.

The efficiency of industry has improved as has the effective use of labour. The government did not hesitate to devalue marginally in 1957 and again in 1958. This stimulated the economy and did not have the wide repercussions of the British devaluation of 1967, as the French did not have a world currency open to speculation. After a period of growth, the French economy settled down to a lower level of expansion.

France has a population of 50·3 million, and a labour force of 20·1 million. The figure of unemployed at 1·7 per cent in 1969 was lower than that in Britain. Gross national product rose by 160 per cent and average income per employed person by 170 per cent between 1958 and 1967. Both these figures were greater than the British, which only had increases of 84 and 93 per cent respectively in the same period. There was a corresponding increase in the gross wage/salary level of workers, with the French increase being 65 per cent, against 26 per cent in the UK.

France had yet another devaluation in August 1969 and this improved their balance of payments difficulties, without affecting their economic growth very much. But their price levels continued to rise, with the retail price index showing an increase in 1970 of 5·2 per cent (OECD, France, 1971, p. 20), and this was partly due to devaluation and a levelling-up to EEC prices. Unemployment was just over 0·5 per cent in the early 1960s, then rose steadily from 1963 onwards to around 1·7 per cent in 1967, and higher in 1970. At the same time the number of jobs vacant rose from 30,000 in 1965 to 93,000 in 1970.

This imbalance between unemployment and job vacancies shows that the demand for labour was for different skills than that possessed by those out of work. This shows a running down of labour in some sectors, and throughout the 1960s the number of wage earners in agriculture fell from around the 1 million mark in 1960 to 625, 000 in 1969. The number of miners also fell, and this will be examined later under regional and retraining policies.

The French believe that the EEC assisted their economic growth, especially in industry, and the rise in output kept down the rise in prices in that sector. But prices rose sharply in the agricultural sector. Average hourly earnings rose some 45 per cent from 1966 to 1970, with a marked wage explosion in 1968 linked with the wave of strikes. Unit costs of production rose and firms increased their substitution of capital for labour.

Calculations are made about the growth of output and its allocation through the French 'plans', with the various estimates of the Sixth Plan being projected into the 1970s. Attempts are made to keep the saving and investment of the public sector in balance. Estimates are also made about the probable balance in the private sector.

Wages and prices policies   Attempts have been made through the 'early warning' system, which had some effect in the public sector, where the State can apply direct pressure. This seems to have had some effect. State pressure on wages and salaries in the public sector has had some of the sting removed by recent agreements which guarantee some increase related to cost of living rises and protects real purchasing power. Wage movements in France should be seen against its growth rate, which is higher than that of Britain. Hourly earnings in manufacturing rose by 8·2 per cent annually between 1964 and 1969, whereas the GNP annual volume growth was 5·5 per cent for the same period. France has a wage–price spiral, like most industrialised countries, but has moved further than some countries to protect the workers' earnings base by cost of living linkage and the minimum guaranteed wage, though she has the problems of high price increases triggering off compensatory wage demands.

The higher unemployment is met by State action to extend the area of vocational training through the National Employment Agency. This field of training is done partly by the State, and partly by private employers. Vocational training is seen as 'an appreciable instrument for the promotion of desirable structural transformations in the economy' (*ibid.*, p. 53).

Germany

Germany's post-war economic expansion is a case study of recovery after the devastation of World War II. No one who saw the ruins of buildings and factories from Cologne to Dortmund and Essen at the time, can fail to look at Germany today as an economic miracle. The Germans themselves refer to the '*Wirtschaftswunder*' and attribute it to a variety of reasons: free competition, hard work and thrift, national character and other personal qualities. But, as we have seen from the economic growth of the other war-time defeated countries, Italy and Japan, especially the latter, defeat and destruction in war has also meant the clearing away of old and obsolescent equipment, the replacement of old machinery by new, with industry benefiting in a short time from the many new technological improvements.

There is also much evidence to suggest that Germany was an example of high economic growth coupled with a high labour inflow into the country. During the period 1949–59, the active labour force grew by an annual percentage increase (compound) of 1·6, which contrasts with a British figure of nearly two-thirds less. Labour productivity increased in the same period at an annual average of 5·7 per cent, some three times the British figure of 1·8 per cent. This increase in the labour force and its productivity was accompanied by a gross investment ratio of over 20 per cent: 21·7 in 1954–9, 23·9 in 1959–63 (EEC, 'Some Factors in Economic Growth in Europe during the 1950s', *Economic Survey of Europe*, part II, UN, Geneva, 1964, ch. 7, p. 13).

Some of the capital investment was due to the Marshall Plan, later to private US investment, and some to self-financing through the monetary and fiscal policies of the German government which encouraged investment. But it is significant that the annual rate of increase of labour productivity dropped from 1959–63, along with the fall in the inflow of labour, a shortage which was chronic after 1960, with the closing of the East German frontier. Since the early 1960s, Germany has attracted large numbers of foreign workers, first and mainly from southern Italy, then later from Spain, Turkey, Yugoslavia and Greece, e.g. some 270,000 extra foreign workers came in 1969. This brought the numbers of such workers to a total of 1,600,000. The sharp rise in the numbers of foreign workers from outside the Community was due to the slowing down of inter-Community mobility of labour, mainly from southern Italy. The continuing expansion of the economy brought labour from the other countries of south-eastern and south-western Europe. The dip in employment in 1967, with unemployment rising to around 3 per cent, saw a drop in the numbers of foreign workers, who then returned when the economy picked up in the latter half of 1968. By the end of 1969 unemployment had fallen to 0·8 per cent, almost as low as in 1966, when the figure was 0·5 per cent.

Basically the German economy is extremely strong and the currency has risen in value to the extent that, whereas France devalued three times (one in a minor key)), and Britain devalued in 1967, the Deutschmark was revalued upwards in October 1969 by 9·3 per cent. This caused difficulties with the other partners in the EEC, especially the French, as it led to a heavier burden of farm support payments; though it encouraged foreign workers to return as they send home large sums of money, which would now buy more in the revalued currency.

The German balance of payments was in a strong position with a large current account surplus, due to an increase in exports in the late 1960s, which was one of the explanations for the upvaluing of the Deutschmark.

Prices, compared with other west European countries, remained relatively stable, rising one-third in twelve years between 1958 and 1970. This may be compared with prices in the UK for the same period, which rose by one-half. The high economic activity of 1968 and 1969 put the unions and workers in a strong bargaining position, coupled with the unsatisfied demand for foreign workers, and the usual restrained bargaining attitudes were eroded and wage drift increased. Yet productivity was high and sustained wage rises of over 8 per cent. Then 'The relatively peaceful wage climate changed dramatically' (OECD, *Germany*, 1970, p. 16). There were wildcat strikes in coal and steel, and increases of 10–12 per cent, which led to relative wage movements. These caused a rise in labour costs, which caused a relative fall in exports, and a fall in the balance of payments surplus.

The German economy remains in a very strong position in the EEC, although there are signs that its high annual increase in productivity has levelled off, and wages are rising more quickly than in the past. There is talk of 'concerted action', a euphemism for an incomes policy, though this would be difficult to implement in an economy with so low a level of unemployment and a large unsatisfied demand for labour.

Italy

This is an example of a country which, after considerable unemployment and a slow beginning in the 1950s, began to expand rapidly. From 1954 to 1959, gross domestic product rose by an annual percentage (compound) of 5·7 per cent, and by 6·2 per cent in the next four years. The labour force grew by 1·1 per cent per year from 1949 to 1959, then slowed to 0·1 per cent increase in the second period, 1959–63. These increases were accompanied by annual rises of labour productivity of 4·8 per cent from 1949 to

1959, and by 6·1 per cent from 1959 to 1963. This latter period was the sharp thrust forward which filled the roads of Italy with motor vehicles and has been the Italian 'economic miracle'.

Though we speak of Italy, there are really two countries, the North and the South, with a high concentration of industry in the industralised North. The South has always been primarily an agricultural sector, with high population growth, unemployment and subsistence farming. As in the case of Germany, it has been argued that Italy benefited from the large reservoir of labour in the South. This can be seen from the unemployment figures in the 1960s, at their lowest 2·5 per cent in 1963 and at their highest in 1966, with 3·9 per cent. The average over the period 1962–9 was just over 3·5 per cent, but the average unemployment for southern Italy was over 4 per cent, with a peak of 5 per cent for 1969.

Italy's rapid economic growth has continued in spite of several wage 'explosions', one in 1962–3 which saw wage rates rising 42 per cent in two years. This had an interesting comparative effect, as Kindleberger points out, 'The response of Italian labour was vastly different from that of German workers. With increased wage income, they saved not more but less' (op. cit., p. 40). There was an inflationary symptom at work here, as workers thought that prices would rise and wanted to buy in advance of such rises. Government attempts to tax dividends sent capital abroad and caused a deficit in the balance of payments. Recession followed, and the balance of payments recovered through the 1960s.

The wage-price spiral in Italy reacts to rises in labour costs which push up prices. GNP rose 5·5 per cent in 1968 and was rising by 8 per cent in the second quarter of 1969, but fell sharply in the last quarter of the year because of widespread strikes, with industrial output falling by 10 per cent. The strikes had widespread and pervasive effects as they influenced other industries than the strike-bound ones. The days lost through disputes per 1,000 workers for 1968 and 1969 were 930 and 4,110 respectively. The average for the period 1960-9 was 1,397 (compare with the UK, where the figure for this period was 268).

The effect of the large wage increases on hourly earnings and unit labour costs can be seen from the following figures, showing the annual change in percentages (adapted from OECD, *Italy*, p. 42).

	1968/ 1967	1969/ 1968	1970/ 1969
Hourly earnings	6·6	9·6	19·0
Unit labour cost	−1·0	5·8	11·5

The high figure of 19 per cent increase in hourly earnings is still cushioned somewhat by the rise in real output (value added) for 1969–70 of 11 per cent. Though the net effect is to raise prices and start the wage–price spiral on another twist. Retail prices rose by 7 per cent in 1969.

The unusual increase in earnings was due to several factors, the first being the agreement between the unions and employers to reduce the regional differences in wage rates (the marked gap in employment between North and South has already been mentioned) beginning the 'abolition as from April 1st (1970) of 50 per cent of the regional differences' (OECD, *Italy*, 1971, p. 13). A second factor was a 2 per cent rise in wage rates due to a cost of living index adjustment. The third factor was the influence of 'the autumn round of labour contracts' whose effect spread like ripples in a pond. There was also considerable 'wage drift', the difference between wage rates and earnings. In spite of this, the balance of payments position remained strong.

The Italian economy is still in a fairly strong position: although unit labour costs rose sharply, they were rising even more steeply in other industrial countries. The problems still facing the government arise partly from the great economic disparity between North and South, and the 'substantial delays in the necessary expansion of social services and in the provision of social overhead capital, including cheap housing' (*ibid.*, p. 44). The 'delays' stem from the inability of local and national government to deal with the problems arising from regional and industrial changes.

Belgium

Apart from the small country of Luxembourg, which can for most analytical and descriptive purposes be subsumed under Benelux, Belgium had the lowest rate of economic growth in the EEC. Some observers have compared the reasons for Belgium's slow economic growth with that of Britain, which is slower still. Both had colonial territories after World War II, and Belgium had a considerable military force in the Congo. There was also cost-push inflation in the 1950s outstripping productivity and causing balance of payments difficulties. From 1959 productivity and economic growth improved, so that Belgium's development was different from its Common Market neighbours. They grew more quickly before 1958 than after, whereas the Belgian economy grew slowly in the fifties, more rapidly in the sixties.

The Belgian economy, like the British and to some extent the French, found shortages of labour in mining and other hard or unpleasant manual work, and had to draw immigrants from low wage or high unemployment countries to do this. 'Seventy per cent of male employees entering Belgium from 1950–4 went to the mining industry' (G. L. Reid and L. C. Hunter in *International Labour*, S. Barkin (ed.), Harper & Row, N.Y. and London, 1967, p. 179). This migration slowed down in the late 1950s when unemployment rose, then quickened as the employment level rose again. Belgian miners left areas like the Borinage and their places were filled, as in the other hard or disagreeable jobs, by Turks and Spaniards, Italians and others.

The growth rate of the Belgian economy, low compared with Germany, Italy, France and the Netherlands, was still higher than that of Britain, with 3·4 per cent yearly from 1950–62 compared with 2·6 per cent for Britain. This higher growth rate was in spite of the fall in hours of work in Belgium by 6·8 per cent from 1950–62 against only 1·6 per cent in Britain (Denison, 'Economic Growth').

The economic growth rate rose and fell in the 1960s, booming in 1963–4, sagging in 1965–7, then a sharp rise for two or three years. Expansion led to higher wages and price rises, with the export industries leading. In 1969, GNP rose by 6·2 per cent as compared with 3·4 and 3·8 for the two preceding years (OECD, *Belgium-Luxembourg Economic Union*, 1970).

Hourly earnings rose faster than consumer prices, as Table 2

Table 2 *Prices and wages*

	1966	1967	1968	1969
Consumer prices:				
Food. Drink	4·2	2·8	2·8	3·8
Other commodities	4·9	2·5	1·2	4·6
Hourly earnings	10·3	6·7	5·4	7·9

Table adapted from OECD, *Belgium-Luxembourg Economic Union*, 1970, p. 14.

shows. Prices rose more sharply in 1970. Wages in Belgium have a cost of living regulator as they have in France.

Netherlands

Holland is a country with a high growth rate, less than Germany and Italy, but about the same as France and higher than Belgium. From 1950–64, real national income rose by 4·9 per cent yearly, by 5 per cent from 1955–64 (Denison, 'Economic Growth', p. 232). Two main factors which helped to account for this were the high rate of immigration and the restraint of organised labour in accepting an incomes policy (incomes will be discussed later). Immigration was high after 1945, with over 250,000 Dutch coming from the East Indies in the late 1940s, a high figure in a population of 12 million. Holland has also a high rate of population growth, nearly twice as high as the average for west Europe. Recently, in the 1960s, the main inflow of immigrants has been from the Mediterranean countries outside the Common Market. Such immigrants need a work permit, which is issued or refused according to the state of the Dutch labour market.

Holland suffered a severe wage–price rise in 1969, their worst for eighteen years. The government brought in a temporary price freeze with the agreement of the Social Economic Council.

The restraint shown by organised labour over wage increases led to reasonable price stability from the early 1950s to the early 1960s. Then the various controls broke down and the cost of living increase of 5·2 per cent per annum 'was among the highest recorded in industrialised OECD Countries' (OECD, *Netherlands*, 1970). The peak year of 1969 brought a consumer price index rise of 7·5 per cent. The reasons given for the sharp inflationary pressure are common to most western countries: wage–cost push, expanding monetary demand for goods parallel inflation abroad and home economic policy. The latter was partly accounted for by the introduction of the value-added tax system, which was thought to have an upward effect on prices: 'This expectation led to anticipatory purchases, which ... created an inflationary climate when the new tax system was introduced' (*ibid.*, p. 20).

The VAT had replaced the former tax system as a direct result of EEC policy, and had been delayed. The government forecast of the possible price rise turned out to have been an underestimate. It was in these circumstances that the government brought in the price freeze, which had some effect on the wage–price spiral. As with decimalisation in Britain, Dutch shopkeepers had in the main adjusted their prices so as to be on the safe side.

Unemployment fell to 1·5 per cent in 1969, after being higher in 1967 and 1968. This contributed to the force of wage demands. The following figures show the movement of wage changes (in percentages):

1964	1965	1966	1967	1968	1969	1970	
15·0	10·7	10·5	8·0	8·5	10·5	8·0	(ibid.)

Although most of these wage changes were due to new contracts which had been negotiated, there were social security allowances, which raised the workers' income.

Control over incomes had virtually ended by 1967 and the 'norm' for increases in 1968 had been set at 6·5 per cent. This proved ineffective and the general price freeze was introduced. This was buttressed by other measures of rent control, stabilising the prices of public utilities and such bodies, and a postponement in the increase of VAT rates (ibid., p. 32). Other measures of restraint were placed on wage levels and the reduction of hours of work.

Norway

Norway has a growth rate slightly higher than Belgium's, with 3·6 per cent increase per annum from 1950 to 1964, with the rate increasing slightly in the second period 1955–64. This was achieved in spite of a percentage reduction in working hours of 5·4 from 1950 to 1962, over three times that of the UK (Denison, 'Economic Growth', p. 24). Labour productivity rose from 1949 to 1959 by 3·1 per cent per annum, nearly twice the UK rate.

One of the puzzles about the Norwegian economy is that in spite of a high rate of investment relative to national income, 28·4 per cent from 1950 to 1962, compared with a UK rate of 16·1, the Norwegian economic growth rate has been moderate. Theoretically, a high rate of investment should increase the amount of capital in the economy and raise productivity and growth rates.

With a relatively small population of 3·8 million, and 1·5 million in the labour force, Norway has a low rate of unemployment and a high standard of living, higher than in Britain. More significantly, the average income per employed person is higher still; measured in dollars in 1969, the Norwegian worker has $4,180 in the year, and the British worker $2,779, including social security and fringe benefits. The growth rate of the economy led to an increase in workers' incomes of 113 per cent from 1958–69. Norwegians claim to be the best paid workers in Europe, next to the Swedes.

The movement of labour from the agricultural sector to the other sectors is relatively slow. There were 31 per cent of the labour force in agriculture in 1949 and 24 per cent ten years later (EEC, *op. cit.*, ch. 3, p. 28). There is virtually no immigration into Norway from overseas, and only a limited movement of labour inside the Scandinavian labour market. The percentage of women workers in the labour force actually fell from 36·3 to 35·5 between 1950 and 1961 (OECD, *Norway*, 1971), whereas they rise from 42·9 to 48·8 in the UK. Another Norwegian puzzle is that while the number of women workers is increasing in Sweden and Denmark, it is decreasing in Norway.

Inflation in Norway was kept under reasonable control from 1945 until the late 1960s, mainly through fiscal and monetary policy. Long-term estimates are made and economic programmes developed. Inflationary pressures have been more likely to come from external rather than internal factors as Norway has a higher proportion of exports, half of them in shipping services, as a percentage of gross national product, than most countries. Rises in import prices are a major factor in raising domestic costs and prices.

The signs in 1970 were that cost-push inflation was building up as hourly wage rates were rising by some 9 per cent, although price rises due to import prices, higher farm prices, and higher indirect taxation, also contributed to the pressures. Though price rises were modest by UK standards, a price freeze was imposed in November 1970. This is further buttressed by taxation and monetary policy (OECD, *Norway*, 1971). But, as shown above, Norwegian wage–price policy can be adversely affected by a worsening of the terms of trade.

Denmark

Denmark's rate of growth of real national income over the 1950–64 period is slightly below that of Norway, with an increase of 3·6 per cent. However, the latter half of this period saw a more rapid growth than the earlier years as the growth rate from 1955 to 1964 was 4·8 per cent. This was reached despite a fall of 7·8 per cent in hours worked over 1950–62. The rate of investment was substantially lower than Norway's with 18·8 of GNP, but the labour supply growth was 1 per cent against Norway's 0·3 per cent over the 1950–62 period (Denison, 'Economic Growth').

Denmark had about a quarter of its labour force in agriculture in 1949, and one-fifth ten years later. It has considerable exports of farm produce and relies much on international trade, especially as a member of EFTA, along with Norway, and with the EEC. There has been little outside immigration into Denmark, apart from the Scandinavian labour market, although in recent years there has been some inflow from the Mediterranean countries.

With a population of 4·8 million, there are 2·3 million in the labour force. As with other Scandinavian countries, Denmark has a low unemployment rate, 1·1 per cent in 1969. Average income for each employee is $3,446, higher than the British figure. Such incomes have increased 120 per cent over the period 1958–69.

Inflation has been increasing in the 1960s and there were big deficits in the balance of payments. The percentage change in production yearly averaged 5·8 from 1965 to 1969, whereas the change in the wage bill was 10·3 per cent yearly with a rise of 4·3 per cent in unit labour costs. Some of these rises were due to the West European devaluations of 1967, which included the Danish krone, but a new PAYE system in 1969 led to rises in employment and incomes and consumption rose (OECD, *Denmark*, 1970).

The government reacted by monetary and fiscal measures, which included action on prices and wages. The official Danish statistics estimated that money incomes rose by 11 per cent, 9 per cent and 12 per cent in the years 1966 to 1969. Wage and salary increases by 10·5, 11 and 13 per cent in the same period. (*Economic Survey of Denmark*, Royal Danish Ministry of Foreign Affairs, 1970). In 1970 the Danes were attempting to damp down consumer demand by reducing public expenditure, slowing down building construction, and taxation measures. This was seen as a matter of urgency due to the balance of payments deficit and the government said 'it is essential that the price–wage spiral should be arrested before it has done too much damage to the competitive position of Danish industry' (OECD, *Denmark*, 1970, p. 39).

Ireland

Ireland completes the trio of countries entering the Common Market with Britain in the early 1970s. Of a population of 2·9 million and a labour force of 1·1 million, there are nearly a third of all employees in agriculture (30 per cent). Unemployment has been the highest among the industrialised countries of western Europe, varying between 6 and 8 per cent, never falling below 5 per cent. The figure for 1969 was estimated at 5·8 per cent. The economic growth rate is also low, rising by 2 per cent from 1950 to 1955, then stagnant, then rising from 1958 to 1961 because of the annual labour migrations to Britain (although this is difficult to measure as there are no barriers to entry) which raised the productivity of those who remained.

The numbers in agriculture have fallen rapidly over the years but the Irish problem has been that the surplus labour did not flow into industry on the eastern side of the country, but moved from the farming areas to Britain and to the USA. Capital has followed this pattern of movement and all appeals to patriotism did not deter investors from sending their money to Britain and other countries. The number of women in industry at 27 per cent of the total is lower than it is in most industrialised countries, excepting Italy and the Netherlands, and reflects the influence of culture and religion.

Given the large agricultural sector and the relatively low growth rate (though this improved in the 1960s), the Irish workers' yearly income at $2,065 was the lowest among the ten Common Market countries, Britain being the second lowest.

In recent years the growth rate has been rising. In the four years 1967–70, GNP for each successive year was 5·4, 7·9, 4, 1·5 per cent. The slowing down was blamed on strikes, falling off in investment and sharp cost and price rises. Investment may have been influenced by the unrest and trouble in Northern Ireland.

Inflation has been progressing at a high rate for the last few years. Consumer prices have risen by 8 per cent in 1970, some of this due to a rise in indirect taxes (OECD, *Ireland*, 1971). The inflationary effects can be traced through cost-push inflationary pressures. Table 3 presents the OECD figures. With these inflationary factors at work the balance of payments was running a large deficit in four of the years, 1966–70. The government attempted

Table 3 *Annual per cent charges (manufacturing)*

	1967	1968	1969	1970
Weekly earnings per man	7·1	8·5	12·1	12·5
Labour costs/unit of output	1·0	2·1	10·3	11·5
Real earnings	3·8	3·6	4·4	4·5

Adapted from OECD, *Ireland*, 1971, p. 10.

to control inflation by relating wages to productivity, and suggested a 7 per cent norm in 1969, but the outcome was increases of 15 per cent. In this, Ireland is part of the general inflationary trend in west Europe. The economic problem now bears a relation to that of neighbouring countries like Britain with 'relatively slow growth, strong inflation, and large current external deficit'. Britain at least solved the latter problem by accepting the first two in recent years and allowing unemployment to rise.

⚔ Politics, trade unions and employers

Western Europe has been the cradle of the labour movement as a vehicle of protest against developing industrialism. Karl Marx was only one of the many who described the process, and the way in which it affected the lives of the workers. Yet Marxism did not influence the unions of western Europe as much as Marx thought that it would, and a mixture of writers and creeds, anarchism, communism, democratic socialism, methodism, catholicism, liberalism, all had their influence in various ways.

Early radical movements fused with the young unions and politics and unionism were seen as twin interlocking strands. France produced the Blanquists and the followers of Proudhon, who mingled with the Marxists to produce the explosion of the Paris Commune of 1871. This ended the story for the French Left for many years, until the development of syndicalism in the early 1900s brought a mixture of politics and economics, and the doctrine of the general strike to seize power, developed by Sorel. The syndicalist movement spread to Britain and had some influence before World War I when numbers of militant workers were impatient and suspicious of the Liberals and the young Labour Party. The syndicalists and the anarchists were strong in France, Italy and Spain.

Germany developed the largest and most disciplined labour party in western Europe, based on Marxism, although the interpretation of this varied between those who wanted to overthrow the State and the reformists who wanted to democratise the State by democratic means. Britain followed the reformist path also, except for the sharp conflict of the general strike of 1926, where Labour's defeat brought the moderates into leadership.

The democracy of Italy and Germany collapsed in the 1930s and the dictatorships of Mussolini and Hitler destroyed the organised trade union movement and created another nearer their own image.

Other labour movements developed differently and reflected the
pattern of their own democratic cultures. One labour historian
summed up 'France and Italy, class hatred but ineffectual class
organisation ... the Belgian, Dutch ... working classes have shown
a remarkable degree of responsibility, although their highly developed class organisations have followed the religious cleavages
in each nation' (V. Lorwin, 'Working Class Politics and Economic
Development', *American Historical Review*, January 1958).

West European unions are critical of capitalist society and in
general, by policy and practice, attempt to change the existing
system by means of political as well as economic measures. Apart
from France and Italy, where large communist parties still exist,
the majority of labour movements in the Ten countries follow
reformist aims in order to change society—even the western communists follow reformist programmes and have accepted most of
the Common Market policies.

It follows that most of the countries mentioned have some
political link between the left wing or reforming parties and the
trade unions. The link can be either direct or indirect. Duverger
draws a distinction between those countries where the unions affiliate a block, which he calls the indirect, and those in which the
individual member joins. Britain and Sweden are examples of
the indirect, and France the direct (M. Duverger, *Political Parties*,
Methuen, London, 1955, pp. 1–19).

The link between the unions and the political parties they support
does not mean that there are no differences of opinion and even
fundamental disagreements. One of the most obvious is the attempts
by various governments of the left to control inflation by asking
for restraint on wage demands at a time when prices are rising and
taxes may have been increased as part of the anti-inflationary policy.

France

It is difficult to describe the political party system in France in
terms of government and opposition. There are a number of parties
of the Right, Left and Centre. Broadly speaking, the parties of the
Right can be classified under the heading of Gaullists, while the
Left and Centre form themselves into loose alliances, if possible,
for electoral purposes. The major difficulty for the parties of the
Left is that the communists are the most powerful voting block,

and this deters the democratic socialists and centrists from entering into an alliance. If such a pact is made, the Gaullists may present the choice to the French public as 'Moscow—or Us'.

These divisions between right and left have been an enduring strand in French history, and is accentuated by the religious factor in that France is traditionally a Catholic country, while the Left tends to be critical of religious influence in higher state circles. The Dreyfus Case illustrates the strong emotions that crystallise around such issues. While organised religion in France has tended to be conservative in its political influence, and has supported Gaullism strongly, the parties of the Left lay claim to the French myth of the Revolution, so that revolutionary ideas are not so frightening to voters as they would be in countries with less violent historical change.

France does not have a clear link between the unions and the Left, for the reasons given above. The political parties are split on economic, religious and political grounds, as are the unions, who are split three ways. The French trade union movement has a fluctuating membership and a weak financial base. There are only three million workers in unions, less than 25 per cent of the labour force.

The Confédération Générale du Travail (CGT) was formed in 1895 from the local *bourses du travail* or trades councils. In 1906 the 'Amiens Charter' laid down a set of revolutionary principles advocating the expropriation of capitalism and approving the general strike as a method. Employers formed their associations about the same time, as did the agricultural unions.

The fissionable nature of French unionism was shown after World War I, when a new grouping, the Confédération Française des Travailleurs Chrétiens (CFTC), was formed, which was composed mainly of Catholic workers. The radical wing of the unions was left in a weaker state and split again into the more familiar division between communists and socialists. The left-wing unionists joined together again in 1936 under the Popular Front, with some 5½ million workers, as the reconstituted CGr'.

The new CGT produced the Matignon Agreement (a left-wing government was in power under Léon Blum) which recognised the freedom to organise and belong to a trade union, and to have collective labour contracts, though there was also a clause saying that the pursuit of 'trade unionist rights must not result in acts contrary to the law'. Works councils were also provided for.

After the liberation of 1944, the CGT majority were strongly influenced by the communists in the left-wing revival after the war. Then the socialists broke away in 1948, when the leftist mood of western Europe was swung further right by communist tactics in eastern and central Europe. The socialists formed a new grouping, the CGT (Force Ouvrière), or CGT-FO.

The Christian trade unions had remained independent but became schismatic themselves in 1964, when the majority decided to emphasise their independence from religious control and chose the title Confédération Française Démocratique du Travail (CFDT). The minority group left kept the title CFTC.

Basically, the three-way split in French trade unionism, and in western Europe with a few exceptions, is between the communists, the socialists and the Christians, though there are non-communists in the CGT, non-socialists in the CGT-FO, and left-wing Catholics in the CFDT. There was also a shift towards more liberal democratic ideas in the Catholic church and the official opposition to democratic socialism was modified by Pope John's encyclical *Mater and Magistra* in 1962.

Other divisions in the French trade union movement took place with the executive, technician and supervisor grades in 1944 and with the teachers in 1948. The first group formed the Confédération Générale des Cadres (CGC), established the right to bargain with employers and to protect and extend differentials for skill and responsibility. The teachers wanted to be separate from the choice between the communists and the socialists and formed the Fédération de l'Education Nationale (FEN). There are some 35 unions in this group, and it is much better organised, in membership and finance, than are the other trade union groups, whose members tend to be slack or ignore paying subscriptions altogether. Education has been a rapidly growing sector in the French economy, as it has been in other west European countries, and the FEN claims a membership of 80 per cent of all teachers.

The CGT claims to be the largest union with some 2 million members, but this claim is probably exaggerated for reasons given above. It is communist in ideology but recently it has been co-operating more with state bodies and supporting policies which it formerly had opposed, e.g. in 1970, communists were given representation on the EEC Economic and Social Committee, and on the Community's agricultural and advisory committees, from which the CGT had previously been excluded.

The CGT-FO has some 600,000 members, mainly in the public services such as the post office and the civil service. It has no formal link with political activities and it usually avoids joint action with the CGT.

The two Christian unions, CFDT and the CFTC, have memberships of some 500,000 and 80,000 respectively. The agricultural unions, or associations of farmers, are powerful pressure groups, especially in relation to food and farming prices in the EEC.

French employers have been historically and culturally more hostile to the idea of unionism than the British employers have been. This has been partly due to the large number of family firms in France and to the paternalistic attitude of many employers. Employers have been organised under the Conseil National du Patronat Française (CNPF) since 1946. The organisations represented by the CNPF have about 6 million workers, and much bargaining is carried out at regional and provincial levels, although there have been signs of a shift to plant bargaining in some of the larger plants. The Conseil of the Patronat meets the appropriate trade unions and state bodies for consultation and negotiation.

The French unions are weaker and less well organised than the British ones, so that their advances have come through political decisions, often after dramatic clashes at a national level. The Matignon Agreement of 1936 was the result of a large, loosely organised strike which brought the employers and trade union leaders together under the socialist Prime Minister. Post-war legislation arose from the Liberation left-wing sentiments which influenced top government circles for a time. More strikingly, much of the pressure was not planned by the trade union leaders, or even by the communists, but arose in a largely spontaneous way. The widespread discontent of May 1968 arose at a time when France, under de Gaulle, appeared to be in a strong international position, with relative price stability, and a healthy balance of payments. Much of this, including the 'force de frappe' which typified France's position as a nuclear power, had been at the expense of keeping wages from rising as they might have done. French workers felt that they were underpaid, employers felt apprehensive at German competition in the Common Market, and tensions were mounting.

There might not have been industrial disruption even then, but this was triggered off by the students' revolt. They were protesting against overcrowding, lack of staff, and the high student drop-out rate resulting from these defects. The discontent and the revolutionary fervour of the students, along with demonstrations in the streets and the counter-actions of the authorities, appeared to touch off a fuse in the factories and strikes spread across the face of France until there were nearly ten million workers influenced at one time. Settlements were reached and large wage increases were given. Agreements were signed embodying de Gaulle's ideas about 'participation' and profit-sharing. The government showed its alarm by treating the strikes and discontent as a national crisis and holding a sudden election in June 1968, which they won by a large majority.

Italy

The politics and trade unions of Italy have some similarity to the situation in France. They have both strongly divided feelings about politics, feudalism and aristocracy, and deep divisions have stemmed from these attitudes and institutions. They are both countries with large agricultural areas, with peasant populations whose economic and political change were influenced either by the church or the communists. In southern Italy the position was complicated further by the Mafia, mostly in Sicily, who penetrated into some industries and ousted or shot trade union organisers.

Post-1945 politics have been dominated by the Christian democrats whose views stretch from the centre to the right wing of politics, and who have led most of the governments formed in Italy which, like France, has the opposition parties split between the communists and the socialists which makes it difficult to form an alliance to defeat the government. The Christian democrats had the strong support of the American government for a number of years as well as the backing, officially expressed, of the Catholic church. This was important in a country where the great majority of people are Catholic, but paradoxically, the communists, socialists and other left-wing groups got nearly half the vote. Voting results of this kind have caused the Christian democrats to liberalise their views in an attempt to gain support from the centre and the moderate left; coalition governments have been formed with socialists as Prime Ministers for short periods. This was the 'opening to the left' which was supported by liberal Catholics and by progressive statements from Pope John, in his encyclicals. The centre left pattern of governments meant that the socialists had also altered some of their views, although their parties were frequently split over foreign policy and other matters. There was agreement on important issues such as the Common Market, which even the communists now accept guardedly. There is also agreement on economic planning, on economic aid to the south, and on the importance of the large public sector, which provides employment for many and directs large sums of investment through its agencies. The largest of these is the IRI (Instituto per la Ricostruzione Industriale). State control over investment and capital in this large sector has helped in economic planning.

The trade unions The Italian union movement, like the French, is split ideologically between communists and socialists, and the Christians. They were under strong authoritarian control in the 1930s. Only one union was allowed for each branch of industry, following the doctrine of the corporate state, which attempted to unite industry and the unions through nationalist ideals and fascist principles. This corporate system collapsed with the defeat of Mussolini in 1944. The post-war pattern of union development was similar to that of France with the left-wing ideologies having a temporary majority. One national confederation was set up, the Confederazione Generale Italiana del Lavoro (CGIL). This soon divided as the national mood changed and the division of Europe between east and west became intensified. The three groups which resulted were the CGIL, the socialist or social democrat Unione Italiana del Lavoro (UIL) which is relatively small and usually keeps separate from the communists, and the larger Christian grouping, the Confederazione Italiana dei Sindicati Lavoratori (CISL).

From a large post-war membership of around 5 million members, the trade unions lost members as there were ideological and political splits. These have since followed the changing patterns of post-war Italian politics and in the 1960s the different groups came more closely together. This involved shedding some of their political ties on the part of the communists and socialists (the CISL had held this view officially for years) who followed a less political path in 1969 when the three organisations joined in joint negotiations at various levels. Since then the groups have met and issued statements about further unity in different activities and there is some hope of a new united federation. One of the main points of difference remains the affiliation of the CGIL to the WTFU (the communist block of unions) while the others are affiliated to the ICFTU in the west.

With these changes the Italian unions are emerging from their political divisions and are adopting a role more common to the 'Anglo-Saxon' countries. Increasing prosperity will probably strengthen this tendency, as will the CGIL acceptance of the Common Market, and their accepting representation on Community committees after years of hostility and exclusion on the part of the Community.

Germany

The Christliche-Demokratische Union has been the largest party in Germany since the re-establishment of democracy in the late 1940s. This arose from the basic law of that period, influenced by the allied powers, who wished to have a democratic system with stable parties, avoiding the splintering of parties which had led to unrest and to the rise of Hitler. The CDU, mainly conservative and influenced by Catholic opinion (although Germany (West) has a majority of Protestants) has been reinforced by the power of the Chancellor, elected by the dominant party. This brought the strong influence of Konrad Adenauer, so that the system was more presidential than parliamentary, a trend which also occurred in France with de Gaulle. The CDU won five elections at four-year intervals, beginning in 1949.

The present party in government (1972) is the Sozialdemokratische Partei Deutschland (SPD), which first achieved some power after some twenty years in opposition as a coalition government with the CDU. It does not have a majority of seats but holds power with the support of the Freie Demokratische Partei (FDP) of Free democrats. The SPD was originally a socialist party and has a long history reaching back for a hundred years. Originally Marxist in attitude and policy, it was well organised and powerful until destroyed by Hitler. After World War II it became less class conscious and militant and became reformist. Much of this was due to the presence of Russian troops and the testimony of millions of German refugees and prisoners who had fled from or been imprisoned by the communists. As Kurt Schumacher, the first post-war leader of the SPD put it, 'If we are brothers with the communists, then we are brothers like Cain and Abel.' The SPD dropped their Marxist policies in their 1959 congress, when words such as 'class and class struggle' were deleted, along with policies of the nationalisation of industry.

With these changes, the SPD moved closer to the mood of the German voters, much as the CDU had done. As in other west European countries, both parties of the right and left fought for the support of the large centrist group of voters. This resulted in the CDU standing both for 'guided' free enterprise and widespread social security. The first principle brought, along with American investment and hard work, a rapid rate of economic growth. This was aided by millions of refugees streaming in over the early years from eastern Europe, and later from East Germany, bringing a willingness to work hard at low wages. The results brought a rapid growth in real wages, so that Germany is now a high-wage country by European standards.

Political ties between the unions and political parties were severed constitutionally in the early post-war period. This was to avoid the political-economic approach of the Nazis. In general, the unions support the SPD, although large numbers of workers obviously vote for the CDU. The free democrats are relatively small, and represent a traditional liberalism. The neo-Nazi revival has had fluctuating success and is likely to die out with the age groups who supported the Nazis.

The German unions are the largest and best organised ones in western Europe. The Allies assisted the growth of unionism as a democratic institution to counter the pre-war totalitarian trend. As the union movement had to rise anew from the ashes, it streamlined considerably. With some $6\frac{1}{2}$ million members, there are sixteen industrial unions, grouped under the Deutsche-Gewerkschaftsbund (DGB) which has some affinity with the British TUC, but is more strongly centralised and powerful. With few unions, all the leaders can sit on the executive of the DGB and work out a common policy and tactics. Unions outside the DGB bring the number of trade unionists to 8 million.

Both Social democrats and Christian trade unionists work together inside the unions without splitting ideologically as happened in France and Italy. One powerful reason is that the disunity of the workers brought Hitler to power and trade union unity is seen as essential for the future. Another is that the communists have much less support in Germany (West Germany will be referred to throughout as Germany) than they have in France and Italy. The Metalworkers' Union is the largest in Germany, with some 2 million members.

There are a number of employers organisations, of which the largest is the BDI, which represents nearly 98 per cent of industrialists (G. Braunthal, *The Federation of German Industry in Politics*, Cornell University Press, N.Y., 1965). One notable feature of the German political and trade union scene is the willingness of the German citizen and worker to contribute to the funds of his political party and trade union. The political parties are assisted by public funds and any party which receives 0·5 per cent of the vote over the whole country can claim government funds. Membership dues and subscriptions are tax deductible. SPD parliamentarians also contribute 20 per cent of their salaries to the party funds.

Union dues are paid as a percentage of earnings and are higher than in Britain. The result is that unions and the DGB are better staffed and provide more services for their members, than do the British.

The largest union, as stated already, is the Metalworkers' Union. This covers workers in iron and steel, most branches of engineering and electrical equipment. Another multi-industrial union is the Public Services, Transport and Traffic Union. Two large white-collar unions are the Civil Service Union, and the Office Staffs Union, with the first having some three-quarters of a million members and the other around 400,000.

There is a grouping of Christian trade unionists, begun in the 1950s, but this has stayed small, and numbers less than 200,000 members. In terms of political stances, the metalworkers, the chemical workers and the printers tend to be on the left of the unions. In 1969 and 1970 the unions have been more militant than formerly, and there have even been a number of wildcat strikes among the metalworkers. There are now nearly 8 million workers in trade unions, some 40 per cent of wage earners and salaried workers.

Netherlands

Religious and political divisions characterise the political, economic and social life of the Dutch, although there is a high degree of tolerance, and therefore compromise, which has resulted in a stable political system. One writer says 'Traditionally, three pillars (*zuilen*) carry the roof of Dutch society: the Roman Catholic, Protestant and general or "neutral" pillar' (P. Baehr, 'The Netherlands' in *European Political Parties*, S. Henig (ed.), PEP, London, 1969, p. 257). He points out that these three *zuilen* affect the choice of clubs, organisations and political parties, for most Dutchmen.

The major parties are the large Catholic People's Party (KVP) and the Labour Party (PVDA). A third or 'neutral' group is the Liberals, known as the People's Party for Freedom and Democracy (VVD). In more conventional groupings, the Catholics are also the conservatives, Labour is a social democratic party in the west European reformist mould, while the Liberals stand for less taxation, less bureaucracy and more freedom in the economic and social spheres.

The Catholic People's Party has had the majority of seats in parliament for most of the post-war period although, as Baehr points out, 'the country is often wrongly referred to abroad as a Protestant nation'. The Labour Party has come close to the Catholic Party several times in votes but has rarely held a majority of seats. This has meant that the country has been ruled by a variety of coalition governments, in which the Catholic Party has always been represented. The Labour Party has been in most coalition governments, except on the occasion when the Catholics and Liberals formed a government with the Labour Party becoming the opposition.

Perhaps significantly, the compromise necessary for the survival of the coalition governments has meant that the militants of the right and the left, as well as certain sectional or occupational groups, have felt that they were not adequately represented, and numbers of small parties have appeared. One of the more influential has been the Farmers Party, representing the strategic importance which farmers play in the Common Market.

The trade unions follow the division of the political parties into three groups: socialist, Catholic and Protestant. The largest group is the NVV, which is socialist (the communists are a small group in Holland), the Catholics (NKV), and the Protestants (CNV). The social democratic unions, who were in a strong position after 1945 when they formed a union movement crossing religious lines, lost members in the later years when the religious groupings formed. Changes in industrial structure influenced the shift as the number of manual workers has decreased and white collar and professional workers have tended to join the Catholic or Protestant groups which have become less sectarian in their attitudes to social and economic life.

The threefold division of Dutch social life has seen a wide range of institutional life which provides funds for the three groupings. The trade unions have benefited from this and the officials are better paid and equipped than is the case in Britain, while they sit on numerous government bodies. Consequently, they are powerful figures, as much business is conducted at the national level and branch activity is correspondingly weak (cf. W. Kendall, 'Trade Unions in the Netherlands', *Trade Union News*, European Communities Press Service, June 1970).

The employers are also split into three groupings, the General Catholic Association, the Protestant Christian and the Central Social Employers. The Dutch capacity for compromise appears here as well, as experience during World War II convinced both sides of industry that some common aims would have to be pursued jointly. In 1945 the Labour Foundation was formed with both employers and trade unions on it. This set out to create the social and economic conditions for co-operation in industry. Trade union membership is some 35 per cent of wage earners and salariat.

Belgium

The threefold division is found in Belgium between Christian, socialist and liberal. A further complication is the language question between the French and the Dutch speaking areas which became a critical issue in 1968. In past years French was the language of the bourgeoisie, the army and government, and the Flemish areas have demanded greater equality.

The three major parties since 1945 have been the Christian socials, who are Catholic, the Socialists, mainly Social democrats, and the Liberals who have been moving more to the right as the party of individual enterprise and freedom. The Christian socials have followed the policies of most of the Christian democratic groups in the Common Market, broadly centre right favouring the market economy with some state intervention and broad social security systems. There are other small parties, including the communists, but the first three are easily the largest in terms of votes and seats. The main parties have a range of opinions, with the Catholics varying between the conservative and liberal wings, as do the other parties.

Differences between parties are not as deep rooted as they have been in Britain and there have been numerous coalition governments, with the Christian socials only once having a majority of seats. The volatile nature of the coalitions can be seen from the score of nineteen governments in twenty-four years, (S. Holt, *Six European States*, H. Hamilton, London, 1970). There are close links between unions and government, as there are over one hundred trade unionists in government, counting Deputies and Senators.

The Belgian labour movement has some resemblance to the British as it is an alliance of co-operatives, trade unions and the political party. There is a high proportion of trade union membership in the labour force with some 70 per cent of the workers organised. The unions are divided into 'confessional' and 'non-confessional' groupings following their religious and political affiliations. After 1945 the biggest group was the socialist Belgian General Federation of Labour (FGTB), but the changing industrial structure of the country, the decline of mining and the heavy industries, meant that their membership declined relatively to the Catholic Confederation of Christian Unions (CSC), which has about 850,000 out of the 1,800,000 Belgian unionists. The third largest group is the General Central Association of Liberal Unions with 122,000 members.

The employers' organisations are, the Federation of Belgian Industries (FIB), and the Federation of Belgian Non-Industrial Enterprises (FENIB).

The two sides meet together on national bodies, the Central Economic Council (Conseil Centrale de l'Economie) and on the National Labour Council (Conseil Nationale du Travail). The former council includes agricultural and other interests and discusses economic questions, while the latter deals with social and labour questions and is more of an industrial relations body.

As indicated above, there are substantial numbers of trade unionists in the Belgian parliament, and their members have been Cabinet ministers. Through political methods they have some influence on labour and other legislation, particularly on the freedom to strike, which has remained fairly unrestricted by law.

Luxembourg

The population of Luxembourg is 330,000; slightly more than the city of Cardiff. For most economic purposes, it can be dealt with in the same way as Belgium. The political parties are threefold, Christian socials, socialists and democrats. Coalitions have been the general rule, as in Belgium. The trade unions are divided in the same way.

Norway and Denmark are the two Scandinavian countries to enter the Common Market. Their decision has been greatly influenced by that of Britain, as they are also primarily trading nations. Although the two countries have a great deal in common, they will be dealt with separately.

Norway

The Labour Party (Det norske arbeiderparti) has been the major party in government from 1945 to 1965, when they were defeated by the right-wing coalition, led by the Conservative Party (Hyre). Although there are a number of political parties in Norway, there are not the ideological and religious differences which are found in the large Catholic nations of the west, although there is a Christian party in politics, as well as a liberal and a farmer party. There are groups to the left of the Labour Party who have opposed NATO and other western European groupings, but the communist influence is slight.

Full employment and the welfare state have been fairly common ground between the political parties although, as in Britain, there are arguments about degrees rather than about absolutes, and nationalisation has dropped into the background as an issue between the right and the left parties.

There is a close link between the trade unions and the Labour

Party, much on the British pattern, and there is a joint committee between the two which meets regularly.

The trade unions have organised some 50 per cent of the million workers in the labour force, although in some trades there is 70-90 per cent organisation. The unions are represented centrally in the Federation of Trade Unions (LO). The unions are organised mainly in industrial groupings, having been influenced at a critical stage in the early 1920s by American trade union experience through returning migrants. There are no giant unions in Norway, as there are in Britain, and the largest are those of the iron and metal workers, the building industry workers, the municipal employees and the seamen, with memberships ranging from 80,000 to 40,000. Some forty-three national unions are affiliated to the Norwegian Federation of Labour (H. Dorfman, *Labour Relations in Norway*, Oslo, 1966, p. 55).

Labour relations in Norway are highly centralised, with the Norwegian Employers' Confederation (NAF) having been formed only one year after the LO was founded in 1899. Most of the larger employers belong to the NAF and negotiations take place in national bodies, with sanctions against members who do not observe the decisions of the Executive.

Denmark

Denmark is also a homogeneous nation with little religious disputes or language issues. It has a long democratic tradition and was one of the pioneers in the field of social security. Both the major parties of the right and left adhere to the same basic democratic principles and there is little argument about foreign policy or nationalisation (Denmark is also a member of NATO). The majority party has been the social democrats (Socialdemokratiet) which has only been in opposition for three short periods since 1945, until 1968, when it lost power to a grouping of the right-wing parties, led by the Conservative People's Party (Det konservative folkeparti). There are other parties, including the Farmers. As in Norway, the Social democrats did not enjoy an absolute majority and had to rely on the support of one or two smaller parties. In Denmark, the radical left moved towards the right and centre coalition in the late sixties.

The trade unions are affiliated to the Danish Social democrats at the local level, so that they do not have so much influence at party conferences as have the large British unions. Conferences are held less frequently than in Britain.

The Danish Employers' Confederation (DEC) was formed in 1896, two years before the Danish Federation of Trade Unions. The members are 23,000 affiliated firms 'who employ approximately two-thirds of the total number of workers and salaried employees in private urban trades', (*Aims and Activities of the Danish Employers' Confederation*, Copenhagen, DEC, Copenhagen, 1965). The centralised nature of collective bargaining can be seen from the Constitution of the DEC which lays down 'Rules for Negotiation with Workers' Organisations'. The rules state that 'Neither the organisation, nor their individual members, nor individual firms may without the general council's consent conclude agreement with workers' organisations concerning: 1. Shortening of working hours, 2. general wage increases (time or piece rate), 3. new minimum wage rates, 4. holidays ... 6. obligation to employ only organised workers etc.' The DEC also receives notice of all termination of agreements, along with the claims put forward. The firm then has to discuss the negotiations with the DEC before a settlement is reached.

Ireland

Ireland is still a country of small industries and agriculture, with 28 per cent of the labour force in agriculture and 29 per cent in industry (*OECD Labour Force Statistics*, Paris, 1971). With a work force of around one million, the industrial base is still a weak one, with the largest group of workers (about 50,000 in food, drink and tobacco production, and metals and engineering next with 33,000.

The absence of a large industrial work force has affected the political groupings in Ireland. The Labour Party is comparatively weak and has remained the third and minor party since 1945 with total votes varying between 10 per cent and 18 per cent of the votes cast. The two main parties are Fianna Fáil, which has been the main party for many years except for coalitions in 1948 and 1954, and Fine Gael, which has been the main opposition. The differences between the two main parties appears clear to the voters, less clear to outside observers. Originally, Fianna Fáil was the party of the poor farmers and peasantry, and Fine Gael attracted the more prosperous and the middle class. The differences have become blurred as Fianna Fáil, led by de Valera, became more conservative. The great debate between the two parties was over their attitude to 'The Treaty' with Great Britain which gave Eire its independence in 1922. Fine Gael accepted the Treaty and constitutional politics, while Fianna Fáil opposed the Treaty. The Labour Party tended to argue the constitutional position and has worked in a democratic tradition, between the two main parties. Recent events in Northern Ireland (1969–72) show that virtually all parties now oppose the Treaty of 1922 and demand a United Ireland, although their views vary on how the union is to be achieved.

The trade unions resemble the British trade union movement in their organisation, and affiliate to the Labour Party, which they support by raising funds. Most of the main trade union leaders are members and are active politically, sometimes holding political positions.

About 50 per cent of the labour force are organised in unions, mainly on the manual worker side, although the number of white-collar workers has been increasing. The structure of unions follows the British pattern of craft and general unions, much the largest of these being the Irish Transport and General Workers' Union, with 140,000 members. The next largest is the Workers' Union of Ireland with 30,000. The other unions tend to be around the 10,000 or 5-7,000 mark.

Under the Trade Union Act of 1941, both employers associations and trade unions have to get a licence from the Minister of Labour so that they can take part in collective bargaining on wages and conditions. Employers are not legally compelled to bargain with or recognise trade unions, but most of them do negotiate with unions as a fact of life.

5 Collective bargaining

The present structure of collective bargaining dates from the law of February 1950, the foundation on which a number of amendments have been placed recently. It was thought after 1945 that the state should disengage itself gradually from the field of collective bargaining and this was the intention of the 1950 law. The state was slow to leave the area of collective bargaining and most of the agreements in the early and middle fifties were on wage settlements. It was thought that the national agreements which were reached would be followed by regional or local settlements which would expand the basic terms laid down nationally, but this did not take place for a number of years.

The major agreement which acted as a pace-setter in the 1950s, as it was not at national level and also dealt with productivity, was the Renault agreement of September 1955, which had been influenced by the Auto Workers of America's Agreement with General Motors. The Renault agreement contained an annual improvement factor of 4 per cent over a two-year period, as well as a wage increase and an extra week's holiday. The agreement was popular with the workers and started the pressure to have more plant agreements of this kind.

There is considerable dispute about the role and effectiveness of collective bargaining in France; Professor H. A. Clegg writes that the effect of the 1960 law 'was disappointing', that employers were reluctant to negotiate. He concluded, 'In France ... unions are desperately and not very successfully trying to push a super-structure of collective bargaining above a state-regulated minimum which remains the dominant factor in French wage movements' (*A New Approach to Industrial Democracy*, Blackwell, Oxford,

58

1960, pp. 43-4). Professor A. M. Ross agrees with this viewpoint and finds 'few signs of change' in the field of French industrial relations, which is highly centralised. He adds, 'There is little evidence of a trend towards local unionism and plant bargaining.' Part of the reason for union weakness is that only 20 per cent of workers are organised ('Prosperity and Labour Relations in Western Europe: Italy and France', *Industrial and Labour Relations Review*, October 1962, p. 63). Professor Meyers (quoted by Ross) disagrees with this view and argues that there has been a considerable amount of progress in collective bargaining and signs of less reliance by the trade unions on the State to legislate for them. He writes, 'There can be little doubt that certain key collective agreements on vacations and fringe benefits have led the way to changed industrial practice and legal standards.'

Recent events in the late 1960s have underlined the trend which Meyers has analysed, and these are shown below.

Progress was intermittent in the field of collective bargaining, although advances were made in the scope of the fringe benefits gained by workers. The 'Lorraine social agreement' in the iron and steel industry (1967) showed a concern over employment forecasting, redundancy, retirement and job transfers (Yves Delamotte, 'Collective Bargaining in France', *Int. Lab. Rev.,* April 1971). Other provisions in the agreement affirmed the responsibility of the firm towards its employees. The 'Grenelle' meeting (May 1968) led to a new wave of collective bargaining, marked by a change in employer attitudes, multi-industry bargaining and other types of negotiations. There are now over 250 plant agreements. National agreements are made in the chemical sector, while regional agreements seem to be preferred in the metalworking industries. Some issues are still settled nationally, e.g. unemployment pay and pensions.

In the twenty years since 1950 there have been over 20,000 agreements signed at all levels, national, regional, local and factory. The political differences between the different federations of trade unions had prevented progress in some directions. However, the French communists have a more flexible attitude than their eastern comrades and while they opposed the 'progress contracts' in 1970, they signed them in 1971.

Consultations arising from the Grenelle agreements of 1968 paved the way for the 1970 Act, whose aim was to give a new basis for collective bargaining. Plant agreements especially needed a new legal and political foundation as the 1950 Act had been designed to assist the trade unions at a national level, as they were very weak at plant level. Between 1950 and 1970 the situation changed greatly, particularly in the 1960s, and the unions became stronger at plant level on account of changing technology and inflation. The intention of the new law was to enable more widely-based collective contracts to be negotiated at plant level, and to reaffirm the right of unions to collective bargaining, which in turn requires that employers bargain with them in 'good faith'. In the past, French employers have tended to place several obstacles in the way of settlements.

The new law makes provision for the 'extension of the contract' by which the Minister of Labour has been able to declare that a collective agreement is binding on employers and workers who were not involved in the negotiations or agreeable to them. The principle of extending the agreement throughout industry has been made more responsive to local and regional conditions, and State procedures have been changed to make such extensions easier to implement. More issues are now covered by extensions such as equal pay, revision of wages, part-time work and training.

Clauses in the new law are designed to reduce inter-union rivalry and splinter unions which lead to inter-factory disputes between unions. Unrepresentative unions could find themselves with no legal authority.

In all, the effects of the 1970 law should be to encourage the spread of free collective bargaining and to reduce somewhat the former strong role of the state in the field of labour.

Germany

Collective bargaining in Germany in the past twenty-five years has been based on the Collective Agreements Act of April 1949 which became the law for the territory of the post-war German Federal Republic. If German workers are not covered by collective agreements, the employer usually pays them the same rates as workers who are covered, in spite of the fact that there is no legal obligation to pay agreed rates unless the parties are signatories to the agreement.

Bargaining is on an industrial basis, covering all the workers in an industry, whether they are organised or not. There is no closed shop and bargaining is on an industry-wide basis. This meant that the national wage settlement was often a minimum one, and pressure mounted during the late 1950s for more plant bargaining, a demand which, as we have seen, was echoed in most west European countries. Employers resisted this move, and there are few single firm agreements. An important exception is Volkswagen.

Wages are the central theme in collective agreements. Wages, in fact, keep well ahead of the minimum negotiated rates fixed nationally, as there are various incentive and holiday payments (the Christmas bonus, for example). Although this is popular with numbers of workers, the trade unions are trying to assimilate these different payments on to the weekly wage.

The German contract covers a wider range of issues than does the British one, and is a legal document containing a 'peace obligation'. This 'obligation' is intended to prevent any strikes or lockout during the life of the agreement. As already indicated, the agreement may be extended to all the workers in a particular industry, if at least 50 per cent of workers are already covered by it, or if the extension appears to be in the public interest, or if there is a national emergency. There are no constitutional restrictions on the right to strike, but unions can be in breach of contract if strikes are started during the life of an agreement. The union can be held responsible for damages caused during the strike.

Strikes are relatively few compared with other neighbouring countries, and most unions have rules which insist on at least a 75 per cent majority in favour in a secret ballot. Public utilities are in a special category and the executive of the DGB may step in. The DGB can also give strike assistance in certain cases.

Conciliation procedures have been set up under the agreement of 1954. This states that conciliation boards should be set up, with equal representation on both sides. Majority verdicts will be sufficient, and if the conciliation verdict is accepted then the terms have the binding force of a collective agreement, provided that the parties have agreed on this in advance. If conciliation is refused then either party can take further action.

There is usually strict adherence to the contract, which in the case of a 'skeleton' agreement on hours, holidays, days off, overtime and bonus pay is intended for a long period and a lengthy notice of several months is needed before changes are made; wage agreements are naturally made for shorter periods of a year or fifteen months, and the notice of negotiation varies between four and six weeks.

The framework of rules surrounding collective bargaining—(a) the requirement that a secret ballot of members be conducted, with a 75 per cent majority of those voting, (b) that the executive takes a decision on the strike after the vote, (c) that there is a system of fines on unions for breach of contract rules—has resulted in Germany having virtually the lowest number of strikes and man-days lost of any west European country. Wildcat strikes are few, and such strikes receive no benefits from the union. However, if a strike is official the men receive a reasonable sum in strike pay from union funds. At the same time, one might argue that it is not the rules which have produced the low strike rate, but rather the German desire to rise from post-war misery and privation, along with a more disciplined work force than in France, Italy, Britain or Ireland, and a relatively stable political structure. There are, however, signs that inflation and prosperity are breaking down the acceptance of legal restrictions on unofficial strikes. Some of the powerful unions, e.g. I. G. Metall, have been more militant as in-flationary trends mounted in the late 1960s and early 1970s. IGM has pressed for more company contracts, paving the way for plant agreements and more local bargaining. With the methodical ap-proach characteristic of German industry, the union developed its own plans for job evaluation to improve its bargaining methods in negotiations during the early 1960s. IGM is the pace-setter for many wage-claims, and their new agreements led to pressure by other unions to maintain relative pay levels.

The move towards plant-level bargaining has been resisted to some extent by employers, and by works councils who take the place of the trade unions inside the plant. The works councils have a consultative role given them by legislation which covers negotiations on piecework, schedules, discipline, welfare, matters which are dealt with by shop stewards and union officials in some other western countries.

Union pressure now is to consolidate such negotiations on fringe and social benefits into the collective agreement, and to gain a greater foothold and influence at plant level. Besides these con-stitutional pressures, unions in 1970–2 were challenging employers and government in their attempts to keep wage increases down to an economic level. Employers were anxious because of lower profit margins and rising labour costs, while the government, for its part, was trying to damp down wage increases to 6-8 per cent against demands of 9-12 per cent from the unions. The government's concern was partly for German exports, but also the rapid rise (for Germany) of the cost of living.

These new pressures may lead to unions allowing more quick strikes in selected firms, although this is technically illegal.

Italy

The changes in collective bargaining have been rather similar to the shift in bargaining in Britain described by the Donovan Report as the 'two systems'. This describes the shift from centralised negotiations at national level producing minimum rates of general application throughout the various industries, to one where the power to negotiate is exercised increasingly at the level of the firm or undertaking, although the trend in Italy is still not as distinct as in Britain.

This change has taken place partly because of the technological advances which transformed Italian industry in the 1950s and 1960s. Firms became larger, as did industrial conurbations. Managers moved away from the older paternalistic style towards a more neutral, professional stance based on markets, customers and the expectation that inflation would pay any rise in product price caused by higher wages.

Traditionally a country of high unemployment and under-employment in the rural areas, Italy's rapid industrial advance brought increased demands for labour which, along with the growing strength of the unions helped to raise wages further, and made local groups of workers more conscious of their bargaining power in firms.

The system of centralised national bargaining was fairly effective until the mid-1950s, though there were difficulties of application as there were wide differences in employers' ability to pay. Employers frequently gave awards of higher wages without negotiating with unions, which was often a lengthy process at national level. Independent action of this kind by employers was carried out without their breaching the rules of their associations.

Between the negotiating procedures of employers and the unions (though mostly linked with the unions) are the *commissioni interi* or internal commissions, set up by law under the 1953 Act. These commissions are meant to have only the welfare and co-operative functions of western workers councils, but they have taken on a collective bargaining role which the unions are trying to infiltrate and control.

The shift to local bargaining was a logical sequence to independent employer action, as well as to the rapid economic growth and the stronger local union groups. National negotiations then served to lay down a minimum floor, and the local groups exercised their market and negotiating power to press for maximum benefits. This led to a pattern similar to that in Britain in the same period.

Collective agreements   The agreements of the Fascist period were based on a form of industrial or vocational unionism which was part of the corporate state. Since 1944, agreements became more like those in the western democracies and reflected the bargaining position of the employer–employee organisations, rather than the power of the State. Collective agreements are based on acceptance, not compulsion, which meant that agreements were frequently broken in some industries and areas (e.g. agricultural workers in the South).

One result of strikes and disputes was the legislative move to get agreements to be binding, if the parties consented.

National bargaining was the main form of collective bargaining, due to the large number of smaller companies who could not match the ability to pay of the large companies. The State, through the Ministry of Labour and Social Security, took steps at times in the late 1940s and 1950s to uphold collective agreements. One of the methods was through the supervision of public contracts for State or regional authorities, insisting on minimum standards already reached by collective bargaining in comparable work. State intervention of this nature was more effective in southern Italy, where State moneys were being used for regional development through the agency of the Cassa del Mezzogiorno.

Wages   The post-1945 inflation affected Italy as it did other western countries. There was a 'seesaw' effect as egalitarian trends raised the wages of the lower paid, bringing counter pressure for adjustments from the skilled manual and clerical workers, and agreements were signed which provided greater differentials.

The post-war inflation brought demands from the unions for increases to protect wages against rises in the cost of living. In addition to the basic pay of the worker which was laid down in the collective agreement, and subdivided into groups (ABC for the manufacturing and mining industries, group T for the textile industries and group Zero for the public utilities (C. Vannutelli, 'Wage Structure and Cost of Labor in Italy' in *Contemporary Collective Bargaining*, A. Sturmthal (ed.), Cornell University Press, N.Y., 1957, p. 236); there was also the bread indemnity. Given the diet of Italian workers after 1945, this helped the workers in hard or heavy work. Finally, there were the readjustment quotas, which followed the cost of living payments and were used to restore or widen wage differences.

Industrial disputes accompanied or preceded some of the national or 'inter-confederal' agreements. Then, as local bargaining developed, the struggles and pressures switched to the particular firm in dispute. This shift in negotiating procedures has been called 'articulated bargaining' as it is practised at different levels or layers: the national, which affects the industry; the industry is divided into six sectors, e.g. in the metalworking industry, where each sector has minimum wage rates and hours. After sector negotiations comes plant bargaining, covering a range from productivity bonuses to piece-rates (G. Guigni, 'Recent Developments in Collective Bargaining in Italy', *Int. Lab. Rev.*, April 1965, p. 279).

The change from the dominant centralised wage agreement to more local bargaining has also widened the range of issues in the agreement. As national agreements had to be the setting of minimal criteria on wages, these were narrow in scope. Local agreements can concern themselves with a number of issues such as piece-rates, conditions, productivity bargaining and fringe benefits, coming closer to the US pattern of bargaining.

Belgium

The high degree of unionisation in Belgium and the long record of co-operation between the various union federations, though disrupted from time to time, and employers federations, beginning with the 'pact of social solidarity' of 1944, led to a stable system of collective bargaining.

Later, in 1960, a convention was signed between the employers and the unions which set out to plan social advancement, and to accept the aims of a high employment economy. Until December 1968, industrial relations were based on voluntary agreements between the parties. The law of 5 December changed some of the terms, Article 4 giving unions the right to take employers to court for breach of an agreement. At the same time the unions have not become legal entities and cannot be sued as such. Collective agreements are still not legally enforceable.

There are more than eighty joint committees for negotiation, or *commissions paritaire*, given legal status in June 1945, which deal with collective bargaining and dispute settlement at industry level. The law of 5 December 1968 modified some of their functions. They have an independent Chairman and Vice-Chairman, and equal numbers of both sides of industry. Their functions include advising on much legislation relating to working conditions.

At the plant level there are three committees for employees: the union delegation, the works council, and the committee for security and hygiene. The union delegation consists of shop stewards or *'deleques syndicale'* whose work is much like that of British or American shop stewards, putting forward grievances, and implementing the various agreements. The works council receives economic and financial information from the firm, and deals with matters such as holidays and works' rules. The committee on security deals with matters which would come under the factory, safety and hygiene legislation in Britain.

The National Labour Council (NLC) developed from the old Supreme Council of Labour, which functioned for the earlier years of the century, and the General Joint Council after 1945. These two bodies were consultative at first, then took part in social and economic matters. The NLC was set up in 1952 with twenty-two members divided between unions and employers. It advises the government, and since December 1968 can conclude collective agreements. Such agreements give the NLC the character of a 'social parliament enacting general rules that apply to the whole private sector of the economy' (R. Blanpain, 'Recent Trends in Collective Bargaining in Belgium', *Int. Lab. Rev.*, July-August 1971).

Agreements in Belgium have become more centralised in recent years and there are a number of national agreements covering longer periods than before. The official bargaining policy of the unions is that of 'social programming', adopted in 1960. The intention was to have co-operation between the two sides of industry instead of conflict, with the workers gaining a share in steady economic growth and increased social security benefits. A number of recent national agreements have been for two-year periods.

Despite the growth of national agreements, there are still many plant bargains, most of which spring from the national agreement, which provides a floor on which the local representatives build. Agreements are now also covering a wider range of items, and most contain a 'no-strike' clause, though there is a difference of opinion between employers and unions over the interpretation of this clause, with the former insisting that industrial peace is a binding obligation for the duration of the contract, and the union arguing that they can strike if conciliation procedures fail to produce agreement.

Wages in Belgium are paid and supplemented by a variety of methods, as is the case in other countries, ranging from time-wages to piece-rates, and various combinations of the two. Job evaluation and work study are used, although the first is not found in collective agreements, possibly for the reason that bargaining is usually done by associations and the factory delegates are usually informed about job evaluation by management, instead of negotiations taking place.

There is also a cost of living linkage with the retail price index as an element in wage increases. Fringe costs or benefits are important as an increase of 5 per cent in direct wages leads to an indirect rise of $2\frac{1}{2}$ per cent. Indirect wage costs are estimated at 33 per cent compared with 67 per cent of direct wages (Towers in *Labor Relations and the Law in Belgium and the United States*, C. F. Seyfarth (ed.), University of Michigan, Ann Arbor, 1969, p. 191).

Netherlands

The system of collective bargaining in the Netherlands has been changing from one of comparative stability in industrial relations, with a highly centralised system of collective bargaining, much influenced by attempts at an incomes policy, to one which reflects stirring and unrest at the rank-and-file level.

Collective agreements had been viable in law from the early 1900s, reinforced by the Act of 1927 and the Decree of 1945. As in other west European countries, the government can extend the terms of an agreement to other non-unionised workers in the industry. Most workers are under the umbrella of the collective agreement, and this has become wider in scope in recent years, as more items were included. Agreements can be at national, industry or plant level, although the latter type of agreement is usually found in the larger or the more specialised companies.

Much collective bargaining takes place through industrial councils, set up under the Acts of 1933 and 1950. These councils can give legal backing to voluntary agreements. There are some forty industrial councils or boards in operation, although their formation has been opposed by the employers in some industries.

Collective agreements are legal instruments in Dutch law but, as in other countries where the contract can be enforced legally, court action is rare and disputes are usually settled by collective negotiation. Arbitration is available, but seldom used for individual grievances.

As we have pointed out, a highly centralised form of wages policy was set up by the government after 1945. This had the support of the unions, and had as its basis job evaluation and an emphasis on productivity. This policy had some effect for a number of years, then came under increasing strains due to inflationary pressures and a growing restiveness at local and plant level.

Inflationary pressures and workers' feelings that their wages were being kept down as a group in favour of profits, led to criticisms of trade union leaders for supporting modest wage increases. Employers contributed to the collapse of the wage policy system by paying higher wages than the 'norm' in some factories and by 'bidding up' the price of scarce labour in the full employment situation. The unions put in bigger wage demands in order to keep ahead of militant workers and wages rose in the 1960s at a faster rate than in previous years. The results showed the weakness of government influence over inflationary forces when the unions decide not to co-operate as, whatever the leaders think, policy is dictated by the more militant or dissatisfied members. Professor Albeda argues that the development of the Common Market, making the Dutch unions more aware of the militant tactics of 'the

Netherlands' neighbours, may cause the break-up of the peaceful Dutch labour situation' (W. Albeda, 'Recent Trends in Collective Bargaining in the Netherlands', *Int. Lab. Rev.*, March 1971, p. 259).

There has been no shop steward system in the Netherlands until recently, and the development has been part of the forces outlined above. Unions had been effective at national level but relatively weak at plant level. By 1970 there were demands that union influence should be strengthened within factories and that the role of the works council as the chief method of workers' representation in firms should be re-examined. As there are no shop stewards, the union spokesman is the *vertrouwensman* who has a passive role in communicating grievances, rather than an active one in trying to change conditions.

The unions have attempted in recent years, with some success, to obtain agreements which discriminated between unionists and non-unionists on such issues as time for meetings, pensions, etc. Differences in treatment between manual and white-collar workers are also tending to disappear. Numbers of fringe benefits on redundancy and retraining have been negotiated.

These new activities by the unions reflect their need to keep abreast of workers' demand. There is a feeling that unofficial strike action could grow if the unions do not develop a more aggressive attitude towards employers. The system of centralised collective bargaining has been weakened, and the unions have not yet worked out a relationship between effective plant and national bargaining. Some large firms, such as Philips, have agreements, but these are rare. Regional and local agreements are now more common as national bargaining becomes less popular. Agreements in the past have been made with maximum as well as minimum rates, whereas in other countries only the minimum rate is specified.

Denmark

Most unions in Denmark organise on a craft or work basis, unlike Norway, where there is more industrial unionism. Collective bargaining is highly centralised and negotiations take place every two years or so between the employers (DAF) and the trade unions (LO). The results of these negotiations set the trend for most wage settlements.

Bargaining over wages falls into three categories: the national rates fixed by centralised negotiations, the rates negotiated by bargaining groups which are above the national rate and frequently lead to 'wage drift'. Thirdly there is the cost of living increase, though 'under the Danish system price increases cannot be used in local negotiations as a basis for wage claims' (E. Hoffmeyer, 'Incomes Policy in Denmark', *B.J.I.R.*, November 1969, p. 350).

The timetable for the central negotiations is laid down in the agreement 'Rules for Negotiation' between the DAF and the LO. It states that all agreements expire on 1 March. Intention to amend an agreement must be notified by 15 October of the preceding year. The central negotiating committee, with six representatives each from unions and employers, meets and selects 'the general claims', e.g. 'those which are likely to be relevant to all or most of the fields covered by agreements.' After the general claims have been selected, negotiations begin to decide the total amount of the awards. A good deal of statistical and economic documentation is used in these negotiations, so that reason and facts tend to determine the result of bargaining rather than verbal emotion and force (though in recent years there has been an increase in the numbers of strikes).

If the central negotiations fail to reach an agreement, the conciliation board can be asked to mediate. Provision is also made for negotiation on special questions. Failure to agree before the conciliation board can lead to joint committees being set up to consider special questions.

Agreements which are reached centrally have to be ratified by a ballot vote of the organisations concerned. After this procedure has been carried out, strikes may follow.

As there are numerous craft unions, there is a well-established shop steward system which is established and protected by statute. Much of their work centres around wage questions arising from the agreements, piece-rates and related issues. Most shop stewards see their work as one of co-operation with the employer, rather than conflict.

One sign of co-operation is the agreement on work study (20 February 1963, Copenhagen), agreed by the DAF and the LO, where both agree that high employment and high productivity depend on each other. They agree that work study is the 'simplest and most efficient' way to finding methods of improving efficiency.

This should not be done unilaterally, but with the co-operation of the unions and 'the personal co-operation of the workers'. Work study has to be carried out in the context of the collective agreement, with trained staff.

Norway

Although there have been periods of strike activity, industrial relations in Norway have followed a relatively progressive course. Part of this is explained by the more democratic development of Norwegian society, and the stress on education. From the early 1900s there have been a number of Acts relating to arbitration and, beginning in 1935, the basic agreements which are a central feature of the industrial relations scene.

World War II brought the employers and unions closer together through their common experiences of occupation and they tried to bring a common approach to the post-war years. The closer working of the political and industrial groupings in the labour movement was helped by the high degree of centralisation among the trade unions. The central body (LO) has considerable powers voted to it by its member unions. It is responsible to the LO Congress for the use of these powers. LO backing has to be got before the unions can negotiate on wages and working conditions. There are some thirty-eight national unions, organised mostly on an industrial basis. Forty-eight per cent of the labour force are organised, nearly all are affiliated to the LO. There are three other small white-collar federations, but their membership comes to less than one-tenth of the LO membership.

Both the employer associations, also highly centralised, and the unions discuss together every important negotiation. Consultation takes place between the executives of unions and their branches, or firms in the case of employers. Most collective agreements are for a definite period, usually two years. Two months' notice must be given before a contract can be negotiated. Usually the contracts run for their two-year period and re-negotiation is rare.

Agreements are both national and industry-wide, and determine minimum rates, which can include personal increments, or standard rates which can include personal increments, or standard rates which reflect the earnings of employees. These can be supplemented in a number of industries by local agreements.

There is widespread use of work study in industry, in order to increase efficiency and enable higher wages to be paid, which explains the support which such agreements have had in Norway from both sides of industry. The work study agreement states that 'work study may not be used to reduce the workers' earning potential during the period of the collective agreement'. In spite of these safeguards, 'wage drift' does exist and can be seen from the statistics to vary between 3·6 per cent in the mid-1950s to 6·6 per cent in 1970–1.

'Wage drift', defined as the increased earnings in a contract period in addition to the increment specified in the contract, has been steady at an average of 3·6 per cent between 1955–62, around 3·4 from 1961 to 1966, then rising to 4·9 per cent for the next period of five years.

'Wage drift' occurs for a number of reasons: overtime, shift work, job changes, but the main determinant appears to be piecework. If the rates are well calculated, there is a strong link between increased earnings and higher productivity. The defects are that numbers of piece-rate systems have been 'loosely' timed and earnings rise faster than output. Workers not on piecework, often more skilled workers on daywork, then demand an increase in wages to restore their differential relative to the semi-skilled men. Earnings rise all round. 'Wage drift' is common to most Common Market countries and the Norwegian experience is not unique.

Ireland

Collective bargaining follows the pattern common in the adjacent country of Britain, with bargaining at various levels such as the firm, the district and the industrial level. Agreements are reached after bargaining between employers and unions, although, unlike Britain, the agreements are separated into the substantive part which contains the terms for pay, holidays, hours of work, conditions of employment. The procedural part contains the arrangements for the settlement of grievances and disputes and the way in which the consultations will be carried out, e.g. when negotiations fail or break down, the matter is usually referred for settlement to the Labour Court.

Agreements are reached with one or more unions, depending on the numbers of unions in the company, district or industry, and such agreements are usually for a fixed term such as eighteen months or two years. Agreements have to be registered and this binds the signatories to observe the terms of the agreement. It also includes all other companies in the industry even though they did not take part in the agreement (this is the extension of the agreement principle which we found also in western Europe).

A national pay agreement was reached in December 1970, which agreed that all new agreements would be for a period of eighteen months. This was to be in two phases, the first to last for twelve months with an increase 'not exceeding £2 per week for adult male employees' and lesser increases for women workers and juveniles. The second phase of six months was for an increase in pay of 4 per cent. There was also a cost of living increase according to changes in the consumer price index. The agreement followed normal procedures for settling claims and agreed that disputes should be settled without stoppages of work (*Industrial Relations*, Federated Union of Employers, Dublin, 1971).

Conditions of employment are similar to those in Britain. There are rates for overtime pay and limits on overtime working. Regulations exist for shift work and premium payments. Redundancy pay was introduced in 1967, two years after it was introduced in Britain, although the payments made add up to considerably less, e.g. 'The maximum payment cannot exceed 20 weeks' pay.' Collective bargaining in Ireland is rather chaotic, as there are frequent strikes and picket lines which other unions do not cross. Most Irish unions ignore the arguments of productivity, cost of living etc., and rely on the criteria of comparative wages, which in turn makes the inflationary pressure worse.

The rights of trade union representatives

As the ILO points out in its survey of trade union representation (*Rights of T.U. Representatives at the Level of the Undertaking*, ILO, Geneva, 1969), the absence of specific legislation about victimisation of such representatives does not mean that victimisation goes unchecked. Most trade unions in countries such as Germany, Italy, and the Netherlands have strong enough union or worker groups to protect their representatives.

Among the Common Market countries, France gives protection under the Act of 1966 to trade union representatives who sit on works committees. Dismissal is conditional on the agreement of the works committee, and if they refuse to give this the matter is referred to a works inspector. Employers can dismiss union representatives on the spot for certain reasons, but the man can appeal ultimately to the labour courts. Employers can be liable for damages for unjust dismissal.

Norway has the same procedure under the basic agreement of 1966. Representatives can only be dismissed if a court agrees in advance, and they are entitled to four weeks' notice. German law protects a worker after six months' service from summary dismissal, and employers can be liable for damages unless they prove good cause for the action (K. Wedderburn, *The Worker and the Law*, Penguin, Harmondsworth, 1971).

It can be seen from the above survey that few countries in the Common Market find it necessary to protect shop stewards from dismissal, as they usually have effective unions which can deal with such issues on a formal or informal basis. In contrast, Britain has decided in 1971 to make such matters formal through agreed procedures as part of the general shift towards greater formalisation of contracts. The same lack of legislation is found on the issue of the shop steward's right of access to management. In most western countries, this is done informally, although the right to consult may be written into the agreement.

Belgium, in the agreement of 1947, recommends that members of the employers association agree to meet their trade union delegates when required to by the latter. This has been stated more specifically in some industries. The right of a union to information from management on matters relating to wages, finance or production, is usually left to negotiation. But Norway and Belgium both make provision for information, Belgium in the case of the building industry where the union has to be informed of the progress of grievances and other matters. Norway, in the 1966 agreement, has gone further and states that union delegations should be given reports on the firm. Britain has also suggested this in the 1971 Industrial Relations Act.

⑥ Incomes policies

The wages of inflation, like the wages of sin, bring sounds of official distress and annoyance. Yet inflation, like sin, flourishes in spite of public disapproval, and for much the same reasons. As we have seen in our survey of the Common Market countries, all suffer from inflation in greater or lesser degree, those with the highest rates of productivity tending to have lesser rates of inflation. But a number of factors enter into inflation, according to whether it is cost or price inflation or, as the economists put it 'cost-push' or 'demand-pull'. The two can be analysed separately, though they sometimes overlap. In recent years, economists of the OECD have pointed to wage-push inflation as a major factor in the rise in prices, and governments have attempted to cope with this by fiscal and monetary policies, and by appeals to, or negotiations with, the trade unions.

In Britain, in 1970–1, wage earnings were increasing at around 14 per cent. With the country's low productivity, this represented a brisk level of inflation. Holland was following closely with around 11 per cent, while German workers ranged downwards from 15 per cent in 1970 to nearer 10 per cent in 1971. France, Belgium, Norway and Denmark, have all had wage inflation in the same period.

Faced with this situation, governments have tried different methods of dealing with wage inflation over the past twenty-five years. The main method used has been the least effective, i.e. appealing to the patriotic or other feelings of workers in particular and citizens in general to exercise restraint or moderation in presenting wage or salary claims. In the previous section, we looked at the structure of politics and trade unionism in the various countries. This is important when we consider what steps the governments take to deal with inflation; conservative governments will try to combat inflation through market forces and monetary policies, while labour governments attempt more centralised control over wages. Labour governments tend to dismiss market forces in favour of greater equality, though they often fail to achieve the ends they profess. As B. C. Roberts pointed out in relation to the Netherlands in the 1950s 'the basic principle upon which the Netherlands wages policy rested was the notion that work should be rewarded according to social rather than economic criteria', and in the case of Sweden (which is characteristic of the Scandinavian countries) 'The stress on equality has been one of the chief characteristics of the wage policy of the Swedish unions ever since the 1930s.' (*National Wages Policy in War and Peace*, Allen & Unwin, London, 1958, pp. 85, 127.)

France

France attempted to control wages after 1945 by government decree, which was legally enforceable, in consultation with employers and trade unions. This was not successful, as the central body of unions split into different ideological and religious groupings, with different attitudes towards wage restraint. Clearly, one union federation could not preach wage restraint to its members while another was advocating pressing for as much as the market, or the employer, would bear. The legal enforcement of wages proved to be ineffective, and there was widespread evasion. The attempt was given up by 1950, and collective bargaining was encouraged as a more effective method, supported by a national minimum wage, which acted as a floor to the negotiations, and a guide to various wages paid above it. (H. A. Turner, *Wage Policy Abroad*, Fabian Society, London, 1957, pp. 14–15.) Turner points out that the minimum wage was linked to changes in the retail price index, a method also used by some other countries. Lower wages were helped considerably for the family man by the system of family allowances, which in the mid-1950s amounted to one-sixth of the average wage for a worker with three children.

The attempt to stabilise wages was not successful, as France was still suffering from inflation in the early 1960s. Discussion on an incomes policy was revived by the Massé Report (*Rapport sur la politique des revenus établi à la suite de la Conférence des revenus*, Paris, 1964) which followed rises in wages of 11 and 13 per cent in two successive years, 1962 and 1963. Wage inflation was seen as a threat to the French system of planning which was in its early stages. It was recognised that wage inflation could not be curbed by traditional market forces, by raising unemployment through the restriction of credit and the curbing of business, which would also slow down economic growth. Economic growth usually brought 'a permanent tendency to inflation' which implied a need for an incomes policy to restrain demand within feasible limits. It was suggested that an incomes policy could best be pursued through the five-year plans, with a 'recommendation' by the government on the 'maximum increase of the main categories of income' (J. Dessau, 'Recent Discussions on Incomes Policy in France', *B.J.I.R.*, November 1964).

Wage restraint had some success in the mid-1960s but the bottling up of wage demands led to a sharp explosion when they did come in 1968. This came as a surprise to the authorities, as wages had been rising at 6 per cent since the beginning of 1965 (OECD, *France*, 1968). However, there had been increases in social security payments and in transport and other public service charges, as well as tax changes which raised prices. In view of what happened in May 1968, when widespread strikes led to high wage increases, the forecast of the OECD in January 1968 was an indication of the way in which the political factor influences the economic. Their prediction was that the higher unemployment would prevent 'any possibility of a significant acceleration in the upward movement of wage rates' (*ibid.*, p. 27). Wages rose twice as fast in the years 1968–71 than they had done in 1966. The OECD Report for 1971 said that 'the preconditions for effective income policies do not exist in France at present'. The problem was still how to control the wage-price spiral. The government hoped to do this by negotiating new types of wage contracts linking wage increases to the cost of living or 'the real growth of GDP' (gross domestic product).

Germany

The economic miracle of Germany or, as the Germans referred to it, *das Deutsche Wirtschaftswunder*, was due less to the freeing of market forces than to the stark facts of devastation by war. The currency reform of 1948 is often credited with the freeing of business and the ending of the black market. While some of this is true, American economic aid helped also. But above all was the determination of the Germans themselves to rebuild their country by hard work. The unions and workers showed great restraint in not demanding the wage increases that were being demanded in other western countries. One writer said, 'when our economy revived after the currency reform, the labour unions put up with low wages over a period of several years' (H. Duschman, *Listener*, 14 January 1960).

This was also achieved with the minimum of strike action on the part of the unions. The union leaders were in a strong position compared with the factory workers who were weak at branch level, unlike the British shop stewards, and the German leaders wanted 'uninterrupted work, steady wage rates, and a minimum of social unrest'. This attitude was shared by most of the working population, who knew they had to rise from the ruins around them. Wages were kept steady by the constant inflow of refugees in the 1950s, who were prepared to work hard for relatively low wages (which seemed high compared to the life they had left behind them). B. C. Roberts gives three reasons for the German economy's stability in that period: '1. a rapidly increasing labour supply, 2. an enormous increase in productivity. 3. trade union policy' (op. cit., p. 136).

This combination of factors accounted for Germany's rapid growth, along with the fact that they had virtually no defence costs, a burden which bore heavily on the British economy. Although in the late 1950s some large wage claims led to threats from the government, nothing came of this. The strategy of the German unions seems to have lain less in pressing wage demands than in negotiating higher fringe benefits in the form of employee pensions, with the result that the German worker retires on a much higher pension than does the British worker. They contribute more weekly for this, and the purchasing power which has led to inflation elsewhere has been siphoned off in the short term for greater spending in the long run. The unions also demanded the development of 'social capital' or the setting aside of part of the annual increase in capital of a firm for the employees (H. Hartmann, 'Incomes Policy in Germany', *B.J.I.R.*, November 1964, p. 330).

The workings of the German 'social economy', as Dr Erhardt called it, gave Germany its high rate of growth until the monetary crisis of 1967–8, followed by the inflationary pressures of 1969–70. Despite a rise in GNP of some 8 per cent in the last six months of 1969, partly due to the record inflow of foreign workers, there were also sharp rises in prices. The disciplined approach of the German unions broke down after years of wages matching productivity and 'The relatively peaceful wage climate changed dramatically in September 1969 when a wave of wildcat strikes led to... increases between 10 and 12 per cent' for miners and steel workers (OECD, *Germany*, 1970, p. 16). These increases led to rapid rises in other industries until wages and salaries were 12·5 per cent higher than a year earlier. The Germans used traditional fiscal and monetary methods to damp down inflationary pressures, but made no moves in the direction of an incomes policy, though this was suggested by the OECD in the form of 'concerted action' (the German Mark had been revalued by 9·3 per cent in October 1969).

These measures had some effect, although prices were rising by over 7 per cent in 1970 and earnings at a record level of 16·7 per cent, coinciding with a slowdown in productivity growth (OECD, *Germany*, 1971). Events in Germany appeared to have some relation to those in France in 1968, when after a period of relative stability, rank-and-file discontent forced union leaders to press for higher wage increases than ever before, spurred on by wildcat strikes. Significantly, the government did not intervene as a general election was near, while the fact that a Social democratic government, pledged to full employment, was now in office, seemed to make union leaders more ambitious in their wage demands. Although the government tried an incomes policy based on 'moral suasion' and 'concerted action' they did not stipulate a 'norm' for wage increases and the unions, pressured from below, paid little attention to pleas about wage inflation. The government refrained from any attempt to regulate wages by central action, and published estimates of future income growth and 'orientation data' to educate the unions. With full employment wage pressures continued, until 1972, without any sign that a Scandinavian or British style 'incomes policy' was to be introduced.

Italy

After 1945 in Italy, the new united union movement negotiated a central agreement with the employers' federation, with the intention of bringing wages back to democratic peacetime conditions. The agreement included a cost of living bonus, but inflationary pressures and rising prices caused this to have an escalation effect on wages. Differentials were affected by this, and a new form of 'revaluation bonus' was used to raise the differentials of the more skilled (cf. Turner, op. cit., p. 14).

For the greater part of the post-war period the Italian government has avoided any formal incomes policy. There were several reasons for this: the now divided trade union movement would not have agreed; the high unemployment in the South meant a plentiful labour supply flowing North; the high economic growth rate brought prosperity and sustained wage increases. By 1963 the labour market had become tighter and the employment level was near full employment. The trade unions were now stronger and in a better bargaining position than before and strikes became more frequent and longer. As in Germany and France in the late sixties, the Italian worker was demanding a greater share of the rapid economic growth. The minor recession which followed the boom years in 1964 did not dismay the unions and they revived their demands in later years. The high growth rates of 1968–9 were interrupted by strikes in the latter part of the period. Price rises developed as earnings rose rapidly; regional differences between wages were being smoothed out and the cost of living bonus helped to raise wages further still. In spite of the inflationary pressure, the Italian government did not introduce a wages or incomes policy apart from the usual fiscal and monetary methods.

The increase in wage rates in the late sixties can be compared with the earlier years. Hourly wage rates increased by 11·2 per cent over the period 1961–7 and by 21·2 in 1970. The effect was worsened in 1970 by a fall in production which raised unit labour costs. Unemployment rose to 3·5 per cent and the Italian government were considering reflationary policies in 1971 (OECD, *Italy*, 1971).

Belgium

The Belgian economy has tackled wages and inflation in a more unified way than any of the three countries mentioned above. The trade union federations are represented on the national committees, and on most committees which pervade industry at all levels. The joint agreement reached by employers and unions at the end of World War II was followed in 1960 by 'social programming' or joint action between both sides of industry. This has meant centralisation of bargaining. The 1960 agreement was intended to stabilise relationships and 'enable workers to share in a regularly improving standard of living' (R. Blanpain, 'Recent Trends in Collective Bargaining in Belgium', *Int. Lab. Rev.*, July-August 1971). Strikes were not to take place during the life of the contract.

Prices have been relatively stable. With the retail price index standing at 100 in 1953, it had only risen to 110, 137 and 142 in 1960, 1968 and 1969 respectively. Wage costs doubled from 1960 to 1970 while productivity rose by nearly two-thirds in the same period (*Belgium, Facts and Figures*, Belgian Embassy, London, 1971). The OECD report on Belgium for 1971 said that the country had avoided the inflationary tendencies evident in other western countries. In 1968 and 1970 retail prices only rose at 3·6 per cent per annum, although wages and especially wage drift increased from 7 per cent in the period 1965-8 to 9 per cent in 1969.

The OECD report for 1971 points out that there is no incomes policy and with the above economic situation it is not felt to be necessary. There are no government 'guidelines' as there are in other countries, but there is continuous consultation between the many joint bodies of management and labour. This is claimed to have made wage price stability possible. Some factors in the Belgian situation are: there are highly centralised negotiations, local bargaining is weak and there are no strong local groups challenging leaders as there are in some other countries; there are sliding scale arrangements linked to the cost of living index for wages, and other social security payments; collective contracts last for relatively long periods. This combination of factors appears to satisfy the Belgian trade unionists who represent the larger part of the labour force and keep wages fairly close to productivity. The Belgian government also have a system of price control, but enforcement seems to be based on 'moral suasion' rather than statutory controls.

Netherlands

Holland is an example of a country which has had various attempts at an incomes policy since 1945. Other examples are the Scandinavian countries, of which Denmark and Norway will be discussed later. Britain also attempted an incomes policy, with indifferent results, from 1965–70.

The Dutch employers and trade unionists, like those in Belgium, made common cause after 1945 and came together on joint bodies. The Dutch decided to face the post-war reconstruction by developing a planned wages policy. The committees created for this purpose were the Labour Foundation (Stichtung van der Arbeid), bringing both sides of industry together, along with representatives of agriculture and other bodies. There was also an economic and social council, with equivalent representation to the Labour Foundation, but with the Crown representatives filling the third position between employers and labour. Decisions on wages and policy were to be taken by a board of arbitration. It is claimed by the Dutch unions that they exercised moderation in pressing their wage claims and that union membership rose dramatically from 800,000 from 1947 to 1957.

Government economists calculated the total size of the wage bill, and distribution was negotiated through the Labour Foundation. In cases of dispute the board of arbitration acts as an independent assessor. In spite of this, external inflationary pressures, such as the Korean War, made adjustments to the 'annual wage round' necessary, which made the wage-price spiral move faster in the mid-1950s and also upset the pattern of differentials. A feature of the Dutch system was the attempt to devise a national scale of wages, begun simply as wages linked to family budgets in certain areas, which later became a national wage structure policy based on job evaluation. Factors in jobs were evaluated and then awarded points. Equal points for different jobs meant equal pay. As long as the job evaluation system merely drew broad classifications between skilled, semi-skilled and unskilled, the system was accepted. But technological changes and labour market factors, differential productivity between firms, all contributed to arguments about the structure of differentials. After 1950 the powers of the board in wage decisions were shifted to the social and economic council. Later still the government allowed firms more scope to vary differential payment to workers. Subsidiary payments of a 'fringe benefit' nature were made, as well as clothing and travelling payments. Incentive schemes allowed some firms to pay more. As one writer put it 'considerable ingenuity was exercised' by firms and workers in raising wage rates above the 'norm'. Wage decisions in the economy came mainly from political decisions, but in 1959, the national negotiations gave way to a system of industry-wide agreements for various sectors. For their part, the employers agreed not to raise prices immediately after an increase in wages. Throughout the post-war period, there had been a wage inspectorate which could inspect the rates paid and prosecute offenders.

The centralised system of wage determination also crumbled under the full employment levels and the shortage of labour. Differential productivity in different industries with varying technological progress has already been mentioned. Possibly also, workers in the 1960s became restive after nearly twenty years of wage regulation and restraint and the national mood was less egalitarian than it had been, and disagreements arose between the Foundation of Labour, which had reassumed responsibility for supervising collective agreements and the Planning Bureau which worked out the size of wage increases (cf. H. A. Turner and H. Zoeteweij, *Prices, Wages and Incomes Policies*, ILO, Geneva, 1966). By 1963 firms were allowed to pay 4 per cent over the 'norm' for their industry, and a rapid rise in wages took place. This represents the difficulty of basing a wages policy on social justice when strong market forces are at work and labour is in short supply in some industries. By 1969, the OECD report on the Netherlands said that the 'price–wage problem' had re-emerged as the principal policy issue. The rise in prices was the sharpest since 1951 and worse than other countries in western Europe. A price freeze was introduced and anti-inflationary measures were brought in during 1970. The report pointed out that there had been relative price stability for most of the post-war period but the wage–price spiral rose rapidly after 1964. The cost of living index rose by 26 per cent in early 1969. The inflationary spiral was blamed on the great increase in consumer demand, external inflationary factors, high 'negotiated' wage increases and cost of living allowances. The major factor may have been the shift to the value-added tax system which 'triggered off' traders and buyers into raising prices to avoid losses on stocks, and prices spiralled.

There was little supervision over wages between 1967 and 1969. In September 1968, the government introduced a bill on wages, which accepted the principle of free collective bargaining within the framework of the 'national interest'. If wage agreements were against the 'national interest', action could be taken by the Minister of Social Affairs, either by a veto on large wage increases or by a general wage freeze. These measures were strongly opposed by the unions and the two largest withdrew from national negotiations (OECD, *Netherlands*, 1970, p. 30). The government also introduced a general 'price freeze' in early 1969 for a period. These measures did not have much success, as by March 1971 *The Economist* reported that average earnings would rise by about 14 per cent, higher than any country in western Europe except Britain (27 March 1971). This was 'despite a stringent incomes policy'.

The home of post-war incomes policy has been in Scandinavia. Social democratic governments ruled for many years, full employment policies were practised successfully for many years (since the early 1930s in Sweden) and social security was generous and wide ranging. Social democrats from many parts of the world, including the British Labour Party, made several pilgrimages in order to study and perhaps imitate. While little has been written on the incomes policies of the western countries, such as they were, there is more literature on Scandinavia, though most of this is about Sweden, which had the most highly developed incomes policy of the Scandinavian countries.

Norway

One important result of post-war reconstruction in Norway was the agreement reached between the different parties, and both sides of industry, that there should be industrial peace for some years. Compulsory arbitration was introduced and a wages board was set up which examined disputes which had not been settled by negotiation or mediation. This structure lasted until 1952–3, after which voluntary arbitration was brought back. For some months in 1947 there was a wage-stop law in force.

As Norway had a Social democratic majority, the incomes policy included controls on prices and dividends, which were applied with some rigour. But the post-war inflation which affected most west European countries had its effect on the Norwegian economy, and the unions became restive as the policy led to more narrowing of differentials between groups on the one hand and the widening of differentials on the other as some groups were able to gain increases in real wages through wage drift got by higher productivity, greater consumer demand or superior bargaining strength. A final factor in the ending of incomes policy was the feeling among trade union leaders, common to most democratic countries where incomes policies have been tried, that they had lost some of their effectiveness as negotiators and would be subject to pressures from the militant rank-and-file workers (see H. Skanland, 'Incomes Policy: Norwegian Experience', *B.J.I.R.*, November 1964). This early attempt at an incomes policy was not notably successful in preventing rises in prices and wages, although the Norwegians did better than some other countries. Given the dependence of the economy on exports, and its vulnerable position in a world trading network, the policy might have had some strategic importance at certain periods.

The reversion to freer collective bargaining and voluntary arbitration of disputes suited employers and unions, although the government made several attempts to centralise negotiations on wages and influence settlements throughout the following years, linked with a promise to try to control price rises, especially in foodstuffs, through subsidies. Cost of living increases have been a feature of most wage contracts since 1945. After 1963 the government made stronger efforts to co-ordinate negotiations and fairly regular meetings were held with representatives of industry and unions. The negotiations of 1966 were preceded by a report from experts on the economic position and the wage–price relationship.

There is not a formal structure of wage–price control, though the government makes fairly successful efforts to influence the timing of wage settlements so that a common standard can be applied before a 'seesaw' effect is created by successive wage settlements.

Denmark

The Danish developments in incomes policy bear some resemblance to the Norwegian experience. Successive governments have emphasised 'social justice' and greater equality, and the Danish unions early accepted the idea of government intervention in industrial disputes. Early attempts in the post-war period to control wages and prices had some success for a time, but the cost of living began to rise faster than hourly money earnings. This situation was reversed in the 1950s, and the wage–price spiral was less rapid than in Norway in this period.

An attempt was made at an incomes policy in 1962–3 when an economic council was set up with twenty-five members to advise the government on economic measures, among which was the need to co-ordinate wage claims and negotiations. Action arising from this took place in 1963 when the government brought in a temporary wage and price freeze. This had some success as exceptions were made which lessened the sense of injustice.

Continued attempts have been made to influence wage and price movements. By the late 1960s partial and general 'freezes' were tried on prices. In return the government tried to get the unions and the employers to 'keep the 1971 wage settlements within reasonable limits' (OECD, *Denmark*, 1970) in order to get price stability and improve the balance of payments. These policies were accepted by industry and unions in October 1970 and had some success, at that time. The escalator clause was maintained whereby every 3 per cent points increase leads to a 2 per cent rise in wages and salaries.

Ireland

The country, in spite of its war-time neutrality, was affected by the general post-war inflation and there were calls for limits on wage increases in 1947 by the Prime Minister. This was due to the 'First Round' of wage increases in 1946–7 which raised basic rates around 30 per cent. Attempts were made through the government to 'hold the wage line' by meeting the trade union and employer organisations.

The agreement collapsed after two years in disputes over the unions' claim on cost of living and higher productivity. The employers contested both arguments vigorously. No new agreement was reached and wage increase rose on a spiral of 'rounds', though the increases fluctuated in size.

Some success was achieved after the crisis atmosphere of 1955–6 with a 'Joint Agreement of Guiding Principles' in 1957, which limited wage increases to a flat ten shillings weekly for males and seven shillings for females. Stability lasted for a period, then in 1961–2 rates rose sharply by some 15 per cent (M. H. Braine, 'Industrial Labour and Incomes Policy in the Republic of Ireland', *B.J.I.R.*, March 1965).

Through the 1960s, Ireland faced a severe inflationary situation, with the rate of increase of prices and costs rising faster than in most west European countries. Unit labour costs rose for most of the decade. By 1965, in spite of a high level of unemployment, earnings had risen by 13 per cent the previous year and hourly output only by 7 per cent.

A report on the economic situation in 1965 spoke of 'growing and active dissatisfaction with wage and salary differentials' and with the differences in differentials between employees earnings and those from other forms of income (National Industrial Economic Council, NIEC, *Report No. 11*, Dublin, 1965).

There had been a narrowing of differentials up to 1959, due to flat-rate increases and wage drift. But in the 1960s the differences between manual and some groups of clerical workers began to widen. This led to wage disputes based on comparative pay, which had a further leverage effect on earnings.

In this situation the NIEC report suggested an incomes policy, based on the need for greater and sustained output and for a more equitable distribution of income. The relationship between money wages and increases in total production is analysed in its different facets, with its effects on industrial costs, export prices and the balance of payments.

The remedy suggested, along with the necessary monetary and fiscal measures, was that in the field of collective bargaining there should be a change of attitudes and a consensus about differentials.

These suggestions made little progress and a further report in 1970 on incomes and prices (NIEC, *Report No. 27*) spoke of no person or body accepting responsibility for inflation and stressed the seriousness of the situation for the Irish economy. The earlier arguments in favour of an incomes policy are repeated with greater urgency and more detailed recommendations.

Several points are made: (a) a publicity and educational campaign to bring home to the public the dangers of inflation, (b) a firm commitment by the government, the Irish Employers' Federation and the Irish Congress of Trade Unions to co-operate in an incomes policy by facing up to their responsibilities and improving their institutional arrangements, mainly on the trade union side, (c) there is a call for guidelines, which could be laid down by the

NIEC, on the increases in money incomes which could be allowed in the months ahead, (d) the creation of a new national forum with representatives of employers and workers which would give guidance and advice on wage negotiations. Its role, however, would be to inform the public and appeal to good sense and the need for restraint, rather than to devise and impose sanctions.

7 Law and labour relations

The acceptance of the Treaty of Rome by a new member country implies that the entrant, such as Britain, would have to bring its laws into line with the other member nations. This process is known as 'harmonisation' and is already taking place in the Community.

At the same time, the Treaty is written in general terms, which may explain why different political parties have interpreted the terms to their own satisfaction. The Treaty deals mainly with economic issues, about which most governments already had well-defined political attitudes, and leaves the structure of constitutional, criminal and civil law of the new member countries virtually intact. This situation would change dramatically if the Community were to become a Federal Union resembling the United States. Federalism appears to lie far in the future, as neither the British nor the French appear anxious to take steps in this direction. So far, the principles of the Treaty have only been loosely applied. In contested cases on important issues, the wish of the objecting country usually prevails, as in the case of the French dispute with the EEC in the late 1960s.

Some laws are left to the member state to carry out, e.g. tariffs, which may be specific in their intention, but the mode of operation is left to the different countries. Parliament already passes laws which bind or commit this country to international treaties or obligations.

The specific impact of EEC law will fall on industry and labour, e.g. monopoly practices, mobility of labour, the movement of capital, government aid to industry and the various regions. An earlier group of laws in western Europe arose under the European Coal and Steel Community (ECSC) which dealt with the coal and steel industries and with some nuclear projects.

89

Harmonisation of laws has gone on to some extent between
western nations; some co-operate on bringing criminals to justice;
in stopping drug smuggling; on patents and trade marks. Difficulties could arise, however, on harmonisation of laws relating to
regional economic policy, state aid to firms, apprenticeships, educational qualifications, illegal immigration. Britain has already
been insisting that entry to the EEC will not have any influence on
regional policy or on immigration policy. The EEC Commission
has made statements about the former issue which show some
divergence in policy about regional aid. The latter depends on
EEC definition of 'a British citizen'. Other examples of change
would be the position of aliens, who are 'excluded from Government Training Centres, Rehabilitation Centres and Dept. of Employment services generally. This would have to change to admit
EEC Nationals' (W. R. Bohning and D. Stephen, *The EEC and
the Migration of Workers*, Runnymede Trust, London, 1971).

Labour and the law in the Common Market

While the Treaty of Rome provides for the harmonisation of law
between member countries, the first and most difficult task before
the harmonisers appears to be to discover: (1) what the law is,
(2) how it is applied, if at all. This is particularly so in the case of
labour law, where the breach may be committed by a large group,
not by an individual, and the authorities are reluctant to imprison
large numbers in an industrial dispute. It is possible to discover,
with some difficulty in a short survey, what the law says, but more
difficult to discover if particular laws are effective, as few countries care to admit that they have laws which they seldom, or
never, enforce.

Some expert observers feel that the legal system of the Six and
the Four are not so divergent as they appear to be. In Britain for
the past seventy or eighty years, collective agreements were based
on social custom and voluntarism. From 1971 they are to be based
on legal enforcement. This shift from voluntarism to legalism
brings the British system of industrial relations into line with a
number of Common Market countries, the French with their *Code
du Travail* and the Germans with their *Arbeitsrecht*.

As Kahn-Freund points out, most continental countries have
legislation which 'regards the terms of a collective agreement as

minimum terms for the benefit of the workers' (A. Flanders, *Collective Bargaining*, Harmondsworth, Penguin, 1969, p. 80). Collective agreements differ between countries but 'whatever be the legal details ... the norms laid down by agreement between the autonomous groups are given the force of law'. It is the question of such 'norms' of conduct being given the force of law which has aroused argument in Britain during the period 1969–71. The absence of law in British industrial relations for so many years had been ascribed by Kahn-Freund to the 'maturity' of collective bargaining. The reasons for the introduction of the 1971 Industrial Relations Act are several, but chief amongst them is the 'inarticulate major premise' that cost-push inflation was caused by the threat and pressure of unofficial strikes, and the unwillingness of unions to act against such strikes. The 1971 Act brings the lawyer into industrial relations, where he had previously been excluded by the mutual consent of employers and unions, and fits Britain into the Continental pattern of labour law. Whether this will make for more peaceful industrial relations depends on a number of social and economic factors, as well as on law, as we can see by examining some of the various countries. Labour law does not transplant easily, and the same system of law can co-exist with different systems of industrial relations in a number of countries.

Collective agreements

In France the practice is that such agreements have to be written and sent to the secretary of the labour court (*conseil de prud' hommes*). Only unions are allowed to negotiate on behalf of employees; splinter groups cannot. Collective agreements usually state the duration of the contract, the grievance or strike procedure, and statements relating to minimum wages and redundancy pay. Agreements made between the union and firms can be extended to other firms in the industry even though they are neither present nor represented when the agreement was signed. This is known as 'the extension of the contract', and is found in other continental countries. The present situation in Germany rests on the law of December 1918, with some more recent amendments. The law makes the terms of a collective agreement compulsory 'upon all relevant individual contracts of employment' existing or made later, and provides for the extension of the agreement to

other groups as common rules. The Nazi period saw the disappear-
ance of trade unions and employers associations in their role as
free institutions, but the older laws on labour relations were
restored in the post-1945 years. Acts during the period 1949–52,
the Wage Agreements Act of April 1949 and the Works Constitution Act of 1952, along with the Security of Employment Act, 1951,
sketched out a legal framework for industrial relations.

Present-day collective agreements in Italy stem from the 1948
Constitution, which gave unions the freedom to organise. It also
gave the individual the right to join, or not join, a trade union. It
restricted the freedom of the employer to stop trade unions organ-
ising, and to dismiss workers for union activity. Later laws were
intended to widen the numbers of workers under collective bargaining, but the effect was to make the government responsible for
minimum labour standards. After 1960, agreements began to be
negotiated which contained 'no-strike' clauses, with these being a
feature in the metals/engineering industry. Recent legislation, such
as the Statuto dei Lavoratori of 1970, has given workers greater
protection for union activities (O. Kahn-Freund, *Labour and the
Law*, Stevens, London, 1972).

The Netherlands, like a number of other countries in western
Europe, passed laws on labour relations in 1945, but went much
further than the other countries in its legislation covering wages
and their levels. One effect of the Dutch attempt to regulate wages
and working conditions was to increase the number of workers in
unions greatly, and thereby the numbers covered by collective
agreements. The Minister for Social Affairs, along with other joint
and tripartite bodies, exercised general control over wages policy
and collective agreements. Sanctions could be imposed on breaches
of the regulations on wages. There are limitations to freedom of
contract in that discrimination against employees on grounds of
religion, politics, or trade association is forbidden. This reflects the
religious and political diversity of the Dutch trade unions, and
also affects the closed shop issue, which can only be operated
against non-unionists and not against other unions, for the above
reasons (M. Levenbach, 'The Law Relating to Collective Agreements in the Netherlands', in O. Kahn-Freund (ed.), *Labour Relations and the Law*, Stevens, London, 1965, p. 107). Collective
agreements in the Netherlands contain a wide range of clauses,
from discipline, pension funds and sickness, to works rules and

works councils. Agreements usually contain an 'industrial peace clause' which, along with other aspects of the collective contract, may be enforced at civil law. But the courts are not often used for this purpose.

Belgium is more like Britain in its voluntaristic approach to collective agreements which are based on joint committees set up in 1945. While many agreements are negotiated at national level, at the local level agreement is usually reached on an informal basis. Whether agreements are formal or informal, they vary greatly in their range and scope. The high degree of unionisation means that breaches of the collective contract are unusual.

A recent feature is that the scope of the contract is increasing steadily in most countries. Wages and working conditions, traditional subjects for bargaining, are now being linked more directly with negotiated or statutory legislation about hours, holidays, health and safety, pensions and social security, while some governments intervene or legislate on wages from time to time. The attitude to the collective bargaining contract varies from country to country according to social, economic and political factors. The 'closed shop' is a different proposition in a country with strong religious and political differences in its labour force and unions.

The way in which the law imposes sanctions on breaches of labour law differs greatly between countries. Some have agreements, either at a national or an industrial level, with a 'peace' or 'no strike' clause during the length of the contract. While Germany has attempted to interpret such clauses seriously, and their courts found against a large trade union in 1958, the British have not been successful in their enforcement contracts with such clauses. The British Industrial Relations Act of 1971 has made the work contract legally enforceable, but until such contracts are drawn up by employers and unions with legal sanctions in the background, they will be difficult to enforce. The railway dispute of mid-1972 illustrates this point, e.g. is Sunday overtime work a contractual obligation?

Belgium, in its National Agreement on Social Planning (1960), states 'the parties will refrain from all hostile acts towards one another during the period stipulated for negotiations'. If no settlement is reached the parties resume their freedom of action. Denmark is more specific and says, 'When a collective agreement has been concluded, and for its duration, no stoppage of work ... may be effected within the scope of the agreement'. There are some qualifications following this statement, but its intent is clear (Main Agreement, 1960, between the Employers and Union Federations). Norway states 'where a collective agreement is in force, no work stoppage or other labour dispute shall occur' (Basic Agreement between the NAF and the LO, 1962). Disputes about the interpretations of such agreements are usually referred to the labour courts of the Common Market countries.

Ireland has a system of registration of collective agreements, though registration is not compulsory. Registration makes the terms of an agreement binding on companies which are signatories and also on companies employing the same types of workers covered by the agreement, though they might not have been signatories. This follows the European principle. There is a labour court, whose functions are wider than labour courts in western Europe, but it has no enforcement powers except in the case of unofficial strikes, where it can make an award binding on the parties for three months, though in actual fact this is rarely done. Ireland faces the difficulty, at times, of defiance of labour laws on a large scale. Imprisonment and fines have been generally ineffective and, as in other countries, made the imprisoned union officials more popular with their members.

Strikes and the law

In several west European countries the right to strike is regarded as a fundamental civic right and is written into the post-1945 constitutions. This is the case in France, Italy and Germany; in the latter two countries, it is a reaction to the Fascist/Nazi legislation which restricted the freedom of trade unions.

Strikes were illegal in France for a large part of the nineteenth century. This was changed in 1864, but it did not constitute a right to strike. This came in the Constitution of 1946, and was subject to the 'limitations imposed by law'. The right to strike was reaffirmed in the Constitution of 1958 (Fifth Republic). Limitations on strikes apply to civil servants, although certain groups of them can strike subject to questions of public safety and public equipment. The limitations are not hard and fast, as their legal position is still obscure. Other limitations apply, as they did also in the case of

Britain, to workers in public services such as gas and electricity. Employees can be ordered to continue at work, but legal enforcement would be ineffective if large numbers of workers defied the order.

Certain forms of striking or industrial protest are illegal; these are political strikes, sit-downs and go-slows; also where the contract provides for notice to be given of strike action (though all these sanctions and prohibitions are subject to ineffectiveness if sufficiently large numbers defy the law). The closed shop is also forbidden, as are unofficial strikes (known in French as *Le grève sauvage*). Until the 1950s the French government used troops and conscription to keep certain services, such as railways, operating in case of strikes. A number of countries, including Britain, are prepared to use soldiers in emergencies caused by strikes in vital areas.

Germany combines a high level of employment and high productivity with relatively few industrial disputes compared with other neighbouring countries. The constitutional right to strike is also subject to limitations as to political strikes, strikes of public servants (although in the public sector railwaymen may use other tactics such as work-to-rule and go-slow).

Collective contracts contain a 'peace' clause even if this is not directly stated (R. Ramm in Kahn-Freund (ed.), op. cit.). Unofficial strikes by workers are illegal if not approved by the union subsequently. The definition of illegality also applies to disputes begun by the union before the agreed methods for settling such disputes have been carried out. The Metalworkers' Union in Germany was found liable in tort for taking a strike ballot and breaking their contractual obligations in 1958. As contracts last for a specified period a strike can take place at the end of the period before the new contract is negotiated.

The right to strike for the German worker is offset by the right to lock-out of the employer, who is not liable for the payment of wages during this time. Neither is he liable for wages if the men are prevented from working by strike action in public transport or other strikes affecting his workers. Workers in the firm who are not on strike are entitled to pay if there is work for them, which may include comparable work usually performed by someone on strike. An employee is entitled to re-employment after the end of the strike, but the contractual position is different after a lock-out

(Federal Ministry of Labour, *Conciliation and Arbitration and the Law as applied to Labour Disputes*, Social Policy No. 20, Bonn, 1964).

As in British law, a trade union is not liable in tort, if it is acting in good faith. In the case of breaches of labour law, the penalty falls on the individual and not on the union as an organisation.

The German worker does not receive unemployment pay or social security pay during a strike. Neither does the British worker, but where the British wife and family can draw social security for themselves, the German family can lose health and other benefits except for certain contingencies. German unions pay relatively high wages to members on official strike, but there is no pay for unofficial strikes.

Italy has the constitutional right to strike, and attempts to limit the freedom to strike have been prevented by various forms of political and union opposition. There are forms of striking which are illegal, but this has often to be decided by the courts. As in France and Germany, the political and related forms of strikes are considered illegal, but there is some doubt as to the position of sympathetic and other strikes. In general there are few clear principles for employers and unions to follow, as there have been conflicting judgments on some points. There is also little or no evidence of action for damages against illegal strikers, though there are recent signs of greater formalisation of contracts.

Belgium makes no constitutional guarantee of the right to strike, but this is taken for granted. In the absence of specific laws, there are few court cases, although some authorities believe that go-slows and other methods of bringing pressure on employers is illegal. In some circumstances employees on strike may receive unemployment benefit 'if an employer causes a strike by introducing new conditions on wage rates rejected by his employees' before the conciliation procedures have been fully tried (A. Lagasse, 'The Law of Strikes and Lock-outs in Belgium', in Kahn-Freund (ed.), op. cit., p. 189).

The 1968 agreement stipulated that workers' organisations must have at least 50,000 members and function on a national level, and be 'represented on the Central Economic Council and the NLC' (Blanpain, op. cit.).

The Netherlands does not stipulate that strikes are legal and, in the case of government employees and the railways, strikes are forbidden. However, the fact that the Dutch figures of days lost through disputes are low, tells us more about the stability of Dutch society, than about the influence of the law upon industrial relations. The stability of industrial relations stemmed from the support which the unions gave the government for a number of years after 1945, when most political parties in power agreed on the need for an incomes policy and this appeared to satisfy the unions that the concept of 'social fairness' was being observed. This support for agreement through centralised negotiation, rather than militant strike action, broke down in the 1960s, when the unofficial strike became more common.

These unofficial strikes took place in spite of the fact that the collective agreement in Holland has the same standing in law as civil contract, and the injured party can recover damages suffered. Parties to a collective agreement are committed to keep the peace for its duration. Cases concerning breaches of such contracts are rare, and the employers do not seem to have relied on the law to solve their industrial problems. But it may be that the awareness of the existence of such contractual obligations placed a restraint on the law-abiding Dutch. The government has some influence on the relations between employees and the unions in that it can refuse to extend an agreement 'unless it complies with the statute. Moreover, when asked to approve the contents of a collective agreement, The Board of Government Conciliators also considers the formal legal side' (M. G. Levenbach in Kahn-Freund (ed.), op. cit.).

Labour courts

Labour courts have been a characteristic of some European countries for many years; a survey made by the ILO in 1938 on 'judicial systems for the settlement of labour disputes' looked at 23 countries in the world. A classification of the different kinds of labour courts has been made by J. de Givry, of the ILO ('Labour Courts as Channels for the Settlement of Labour Disputes', *B.J.I.R.*, November 1968). He makes a distinction between 'legal disputes' or 'disputes over rights' and 'economic disputes'. The first is concerned with what the British call procedural rules, and the second with substantive issues.

French labour courts (*conseils de prud'hommes*) were set up to

deal with individual labour disputes, but this became increasingly
the collective labour dispute. In Germany the labour courts are
said by de Givry to have a role similar to the US system. The
German courts have jurisdiction on disputes over rights. Their
scope has been extended as the volume of case law has increased
over the years. Belgium set up labour courts in 1967. Courts dealing with disputes over rights contained in collective agreements are
found in the Scandinavian countries.

The proceedings in these courts is usually guided by a professional lawyer who acts as chairman, although he is flanked by
two lay members representing employers' and workers' sides respectively. These are sometimes known as 'wingmen'. Although it
might be thought that the composition of the court would lead to
partisan disputes and split voting, agreement is reached in over
98 per cent of cases examined in one survey (W. H. McPherson
and F. Meyers, *French Labour Courts: Judgment by Peers*, University of Illinois Press, 1966).

Germany has a system of lower and higher labour courts. The
former have usually two laymen and from one to three professional
judges. The payment which the wingmen receive for time lost is
minimal (B. Aaron, *Labour Courts*, UCLA Press, Reprint no. 209,
1970, p. 854), and people are reluctant to sit as 'wingmen'. The situation in Britain seems to be different, as there is no shortage of
wingmen (although the TUC has recommended a boycott by trade
union officials of the new Industrial Tribunals, which may have
an effect on the balance of the tribunals).

The French, German and Belgian labour courts have an obligation to settle the dispute by compromise if possible. This gives the
parties an opportunity of assessing the strength of the opposing
case, and possibly the view of the conciliators, one employer and
one employee each acting alternately as chairman (Aaron, op. cit.,
p. 860). For Germany, Professor Ramm estimates that '30 to 40
per cent of the cases filed with the lower labour courts are settled
by compromise' (*ibid.*, p. 862).

One feature of the French and German labour courts is that they
are far less expensive than in comparable tribunals in the USA
(J. Fleming in Aaron, op. cit.). The chief reason for this is the cost
of legal representation in the US, which is less frequent and less
costly in the two countries mentioned. The French *conseil de
prud'hommes* is made up of both employers and workers with no

legal chairman. This keeps down the cost of proceedings. It may be that the British Industrial Relations Act will make industrial tribunal and court cases more costly than at present if firms use lawyers and unions follow suit.

Norway's Labour Disputes Act dates from 1915 and appears to have been accepted by employers and workers for most of that time. As in the west European countries we have examined, a distinction is made between disputes of 'right' and disputes of 'interest', and the disputes of 'right' are referred to the labour court for decisive settlement. Conflicts about 'interest' go to mediation, and, failing settlement, strikes may occur.

The labour court consists of seven members, two each nominated by employers and workers, and three 'anchormen': the chairman and two others who fill the neutral role between the two sides. Of the three neutrals, two are highly qualified lawyers. Local labour disputes can be dealt with by the local law courts, where judges are flanked by a nominee each from employers and workers. The labour courts will try to conciliate before the case where majority voting can establish the verdict. The decision becomes case law as in other countries (H. Dorfman, *Labour Relations in Norway*, Ministry of Foreign Affairs, Oslo, 1965).

The labour court of Denmark was set up in 1919 and the revised Act of 1964 says that the court shall have six members and sixteen substitute members, a president and three vice-presidents. Three members and eight substitutes are nominated separately by the Danish Employers' Confederation and the Danish Federation of Trade Unions. The president, vice-presidents, and one of three nominees from each side, as well as substitutes, must have legal qualifications. The costs of the court, including the fees and subsistence allowances, are met by the State.

Such courts deal with breaches of agreements by either workers or employers. Action can be taken by the court on either strikes or lock-outs as the following rule shows:

7. Similarly, when a workers' organisation or members' thereof in conflict with the existing agreements, board of arbitration awards or a judgement of the Court, initiate or persist in a strike against the employers' organisation or members thereof or an individual undertaking, the employers' organisation or the individual undertaking may summon the workers' organisation

before the Labour Court (*The Labour Court*, Ministry of Labour, Oslo, 1964).

The labour court can impose fines, and can command witnesses to appear. It does not attempt to by-pass arbitration and insists that 'It shall be regarded as a particularly aggravating circumstance if the party breaking the agreement has refused to allow the dispute to go to arbitration, although bound by agreement to do so' (*ibid.*).

In practice employers seldom take workers before the labour court in Norway. This is partly due to the absence of serious conflict. When action is taken and the workers found to be in the wrong, the employer often does not insist on damages but rests satisfied in having his legal position or action legally confirmed.

The Irish labour court is an independent body set up by the 1946 Industrial Relations Act. Representatives of both employers and trade unions sit on the court, with neutral chairman and deputy chairman.

The court takes action in a dispute when it has gone through the collective bargaining machinery and both sides decide to ask for the dispute to be heard. Disputes can also be referred to the court if the trade union requests and agrees to accept the judgment, 'or if both parties agree to accept the Recommendation of the court on a specified issue. Such investigations are always private.' Apart from this the recommendations of the court are not binding. The court does not have the legal authority of a court of law. Proceedings are informal and a party to a dispute may refuse to appear and give evidence, e.g. in a case of 22 March 1971, 'Pay of female clerical workers'. The company refused to appear and the labour court felt that it would be 'a waste of time' to ask them to submit 'information or arguments ... or to co-operate ... it was obvious that the Company would not be prepared to accept any detailed Recommendation from the Court' ('Labour Court Recommendations' in *Trade Union Information*, Irish Congress of Trade Unions (ICTU), Dublin, April 1971).

In spite of the difficulties of persuading recalcitrant parties to carry out the recommendations, the labour court achieved their acceptance by workers in some 75 per cent of the recommendations made. Even where there were rejections of recommendations (twenty-one cases), only three work stoppages resulted from these

('Labour Court Report', *Trade Union Information*, ICTU, Dublin, 1970, October-November 1971).

Industrial relations officers are appointed by the labour court. They assist at conciliation proceedings; any party to a dispute can ask for the conciliation service to assist in a settlement. Conciliation works in the same way as in other west European countries, notably Britain, with the official holding discussions and making suggestions. The labour court claim that three-quarters of disputes dealt with yearly by the conciliation service are settled.

One feature of the Irish industrial relations scene is that the Minister of Labour appoints a Rights Commissioner, who has been described by some as an industrial ombudsman, to look at disputes and report if parties should appeal to the labour court.

The court combines in itself a number of functions which were done in Britain in 1965-70 by different bodies: conciliation, arbitration, procedure agreements, the registration of agreements and the formation of joint industrial councils. The court's industrial relations officers can assist in improving collective agreements and defining procedures.

Table 4 *Industrial disputes*

| | | | | *No. of days lost per 1,000 persons employed* | |
| | | | | *Average for* | |
Country	*1969*	*1970*	*5 Years 1961-5*	*5 Years 1966-70*	*10 Years 1961-70*
France	200	190	340	265(a)	306(b)
Germany	20	10	34	12	23
Italy	4,110	1,500	1,200	966	1,093
Belgium	100	870	130	322	226
Netherlands	10	140	16	34	25
Norway		70	212	18	115
Denmark	70	160	768	60	414
Ireland	2,150	480	1,002	1,096	1,049
UK	520	740	238	404	321

(a) and (b). These figures omit 1968 which was a year of large-scale, semi-political strikes in France.
Adapted from *Department of Employment Gazette*, December 1971, p. 1167.

Agreements can be registered with the court. Negotiations are still left to the parties concerned, as is the settlement of disputes. But 'it discourages lightning strikes and gives a reasonable reassurance that disputes will be settled by negotiation.' Registration means an undertaking that 'a firm procedure should be specified in the agreement.'

The figures in Table 4 are not strictly comparable for a number of reasons, but they are based on the mining, manufacturing, construction and transport industries, and provide a fair sample of trends. The figures show that labour in most countries has been becoming rather more militant and strike prone. In 1970 all countries in the table, excepting France, Germany, Italy and Ireland, had higher figures than the previous year. Italy, Belgium, Netherlands, Ireland and UK, show a rising number of days lost in the second half of the sixties.

⑧ Industrial democracy

Historically, the French were among the founders of industrial democracy. St-Simon, Proudhon and Fournier wrote much on the subject, and the self-governing workshop appeared first in France.

Yet the main stream of radical labour has by-passed this development, and the French syndicalists were influenced by Sorel towards industrial action aimed at overturning the State. In contrast to the Scandinavian countries, Britain and Holland, France has a large Communist-led union movement which has resulted in a sharper confrontation between workers and employers than in neighbouring countries.

The French equivalent of the works council is the *comité d'entreprise*. This was created by the law of February 1945, which was carried through on the tide of post-liberation reform. This says that *comités d'entreprise* are to be established in undertakings of fifty or more workers in the private sector. Secret elections are provided for. Similar arrangements exist in the public sector, where the committees are more firmly based. Unions can send a member as observer, and members are allowed twenty hours' paid time monthly to carry out their work.

As in other countries, the role of the committee is consultative, but the law states that information should be given on redundancy, rules of work, and profit distribution, also on matters relating to the firm's performance, such as turnover, wages, productivity, etc.

Although industrial democracy has been repeatedly demanded from the left wing, and often opposed by employers in west European countries as usurping managerial authority and property rights, there is a centre-right point of view based on Catholic social thought which favours participation.

103

The French riots of 1968 set off a number of demands for greater participation in the enterprise. General de Gaulle made a number of speeches on this theme but his definitions were vague, and apart from saying that workers have to be involved in the decisions which concern them, and that regular meetings should be arranged, the most concrete result was a number of profit-sharing schemes. Those schemes owe more to government support than to trade union reaction, which varied from the criticism of the communist CGT and the more cautious approach of the socialist CGT-FO, to a guarded acceptance.

Profit-sharing The Ordinance of August 1967 set out the principle that it is 'essential that employers and wage and salary earners, who together further the development of firms, should share the reward of their joint efforts' (Ambassade de France, *French Worker Participation in Profit-Sharing*). This will apply to firms of over 100 employees. As it is optional below this size and the majority of firms are small, it will apply to some two million employees (15 per cent).

The main application is the setting-up of a 'special worker participation reserve', formed by keeping a part of the yearly profits (the taxable profit). This is distributed in relation to the wage or salary of the worker, within specified limits (so that senior managers get proportionally less). The reserve may be allocated as: (a) company shares, (b) an investment fund inside the firm, (c) outside investment funds in transferable securities. Payment of such funds is to take place at the end of five years, though special withdrawals are possible in emergencies.

The objectives are to stimulate savings, investment and participation by the workers. The firm benefits by tax relief on profits, or 50 per cent of the amount paid into the reserve fund. Employers and workers discuss the range of saving and investment which is possible. The gains are small, amounting to a few per cent of the yearly wages bill, but will increase with economic and financial growth.

Three results are expected: the employee will have 'a stake in the firm' and will take greater interest in its efficiency and fortunes; participation will increase and become more responsible, though the French government says that this is not intended to become joint management but 'a dialogue'; nationally, the measure would have an anti-inflationary effect, as it would apply to the larger companies, who are the pace-makers in comparative wage claims. The public sector has yet to find a method for those areas where there is no measure of profit. But some, e.g. Renault, have promoted bills on shareholding since December 1969. In this case three-quarters of the shares remain the property of the State, which has the majority of seats on the board of directors. Shares are distributed on a basis of seniority and responsibility in the firm. Workers can keep their shares when they leave the firms, and they can be passed on to near relatives.

Recognition of the union's right to bargain inside a firm did not come in France until December 1968, and stemmed from the 'events' or 'troubles' of May 1968. A number of large firms in the car, chemicals and aeronautics industry recognised these rights before the Bill was passed, and allowed the unions numbers of delegates, and time to conduct union business and discuss wages. Most firms waited for the law to lay down hours of work, numbers and functions of delegates.

Before 1968, the legal position stemmed from April 1946, which provided for *délégués du personnel* to be elected by ballot in firms of at least ten employees. The *délégué* can be compared to the British shop steward, though his responsibilities are wider as he has rights of consultation and access to the *Inspecteur du Travail*. Like their British counterparts the *délégués du personnel* have some protection from dismissal but their numbers and interest fluctuate.

France is a rather stratified society and opportunities for promotion in the enterprise appear limited. There is greater polarisation of attitudes between employers and workers than in Germany or Holland and it is significant that reforms achieved in other countries by negotiation have been introduced in France by legislation. As laws can only alter industrial relations where both parties co-operate in implementing or observing them, the legal situation is still obscure in some areas.

Germany

The belief in discipline and order which is still evident in German life, runs like a thread through the industrial relations system. As in the case of France, there has been legislation about workers representation since World War I. The post-war Weimar Republic introduced the 1920 Works Councils Act for undertakings of twenty or more workers. These councils were wiped out, as was the democratic union movement, by the Nazis in 1933.

Works councils were brought back under the Industrial Constitutions Act of 1952. They can be set up in any enterprise with over five employees. Matters discussed include starting and finishing times, holidays, piece-rates, welfare. The intention is that these matters should be decided jointly, but at times this is interpreted as only the right to be consulted. In larger companies there are industrial committees which can play a more decisive part in production, finance and general operation. The board of directors may have up to one-third employees (*Social Conditions and Social Security*, Federal German Embassy, London, 1968, p. 34).

Works councils can negotiate on wages and working conditions if these are not usually covered by a collective agreement. There is access from the council to the labour court for certain issues. There are elections in the factory or plant for the council but Sturmthal says there is little turnover and mentions the existence of the 'professional works councillor' (A. Sturmthal, *Workers Councils*, Harvard University Press, Cambridge, Mass., 1963. This book contains a detailed analysis of several countries in east and west Europe).

A more fundamental change in employee–employer relations was the Co-determination (*Mitbestimmurg*) Act of 1951, which dealt mainly with mining and steel. The board of directors is made up of equal numbers of employers and workers, with a 'neutral' agreed by both sides. The Act provided for the appointment of a labour director who is a member of the board, acceptable to both parties and deals mainly with social and personnel policies. The majority of labour directors seem to have risen from the shop floor, as Furstenberg states that 68 per cent had only a primary school education and as few as 9 per cent had a university education. 29 per cent had been trained as skilled workers, but most had occupied responsible posts, from foreman to managing clerk, or trade union official (23 per cent) in their work career. In 1968 there were 71 directors (F. Furstenberg, 'Workers' Participation in Management in the Federal Republic of Germany', *International Institute for Labour Studies Bulletin No. 6*, June 1969, p. 120).

Most of the issues in co-determination relate to social and welfare matters, although manpower issues, redundancy, recruitment, and technological change, are discussed. The trade unions play an important role in co-determination, as they do on the works councils, where some 80 per cent belong to the DGB.

Although workers' participation has been in operation for some twenty years, a number of employers are still resistant to it, and trade unionists are critical or sceptical of its benefits. The more traditional employers argue that the job of management is to manage and that their responsibilities are the efficiency and profitability of the firm and the interest of its shareholders. The unions argue that participation in industrial decisions is as much a right as is the right to vote and be consulted in political decisions. The unions want to extend and deepen the area of co-determination.

Surveys of German workers have shown that, while most of them knew that co-determination took place in their undertaking, only half had any definite idea as to its purpose and only one in ten 'had some knowledge of the actual composition of the Supervisory Board' (Furstenberg, op. cit., p. 130). This reinforces the Norwegian surveys which showed that most workers' ideas of participation related to the work group or job area.

British thinking on co-determination views is as neutral in its effect. The Donovan Commission stated that there was disagreement as to its effectiveness, and noted that 'the structure of the coal and steel boards was particularly unwelcome to most employers and strongly defended by most trade unionists' (Cmnd 3623, p. 258). The Commission was also critical of profit-sharing and co-partnership, concluding 'such schemes cannot be an acceptable substitute for the reform of industrial relations through comprehensive factory and company agreements' (ibid., p. 260).

Italy

Works councils in Italy are known as *'commissione interi'*, translated as internal commissions (though one American writer calls them grievance committees). One of the first was set up in 1903 at Itala automobile plant in Turin. All complaints and grievances had to be considered by the committee and resolved, or sent to arbitration. However, in the militant spirit of the period, the agreement did not last long, though the works council idea became one of the aims of organised labour.

The councils were re-established after World War I, as they were in other west European countries. They vanished in their democratic form with the post-war revolutionary upsurge and the many strikes, which led to the Fascists coming to power, and the supremacy of Fascist syndicalism and the principle of the corporate state. Strikes and lock-outs were forbidden in the public sector, while labour courts were created to judge on dispute in the private sector. Organisation consisted of one employers' organisation and one workers' organisation for each industry.

The defeat of Fascism in 1944 revived an old demand for workers' control of factories. Committees of liberation or administration were set up in various factories. The Christian democrats and many employers resisted the more extreme forms of workers' control and numbers of internal councils functioned only with the consent of management.

An agreement of August 1947 gave internal commissions a new status and functions, but disagreement on the part of the unions led to matters being settled by negotiation instead of by statutory law. The point of issue was the fear of unemployment and dismissals, and the fact that the commissions might take the place of the unions in discussing and ruling on dismissals. After 1950 the unions began to use the commissions as a direct channel for union influence, although the existence of Christian, communist and socialist unions led to active electoral contests for commission membership based on the different ideologies of the unions.

Belgium

Factory councils (*conseils d'entreprise*) were set up by law in September 1948. The intention of the Act was to begin regular and systematic consultation between employers and employees. Undertakings with an average workforce of fifty or more may have a council, while those with more than 150 workers must have one. Their functions are to discuss and make recommendations about social legislation, work regulations and more fundamentally, about the methods used by management to change organisation or output. Employers must give necessary information to the factory councils on economic and financial matters.

The size of the council representation for workers varies from four members for the smaller firms to eighteen in a workforce of over 6,000. This makes the membership of councils range from eight to thirty-six as management provide matching numbers. Election is by all workers in the firm. Councils cannot be set up in a factory which has no union. This is designed to prevent employers helping to introduce a factory council as a means of preventing unionisation. Meetings are held about once a month.

Disputes arising from the councils are submitted to a joint labour management commission (*commission paritaire*). Model agendas for factory councils are drawn up by the commissions. The *commissions paritaires* were also set up by law in the immediate postwar period (June 1945) and supplemented in March 1954. The commissions deal with collective bargaining in industries, or sectors of industries. There are at least four members representing workers or staff sides, nominated by their respective unions or associations (A. Delperee, 'Joint Committees in Belgium', *Int. Lab. Rel.*, No. 3, 1960). Decisions are made by agreement. The commission discusses a wide range of issues which are usually found in collective agreements, ranging from pay to conditions of work, from apprenticeships to social legislation.

Greater powers were given to the factory councils in 1967, with the aim of encouraging greater participation.

Netherlands

The Dutch system, like the various coalition governments, is based on a good deal of compromise, and there are less ideological differences between employers and employees than in most west European countries. This is partly due to the strong religious background, as both Protestant and Catholic groups have exercised an influence on industrial life.

The Works Council Act was passed in 1950, and is framed to emphasise that industry is a joint or co-operative effort, to 'help to ensure the satisfactory running of the undertaking'. Councils are joint bodies drawn from the workers. Most of the issues discussed relate to welfare, holidays, piece-work, etc., and the councils leave negotiation on wages and related issues to the unions.

There is no system of co-determination as in Germany, but in 1960, after the Dutch unions had expressed dissatisfaction with the powers of works councils, the government appointed a commission which reported in 1964. The recommendations moved some way towards the German system, saying that the board of supervisory directors, which represents shareholders, should have an employee member. In 1968 the Social Economic Council, a tripartite body, approved a Bill for a Works Council Act (R. Nolen, 'Co-determination and Participation in the Netherlands', in *Co-partnership*, The Industrial Co-Partnership Association, London, July 1970, p. 25) which was intended to give more powers to workers' representatives, reflecting the more militant mood of the unions. The functions of the works councils are consultative, not executive. A list of subjects which may be discussed by the employees are laid down in the 1950 Act. The employer has to be chairman of the works council, whose size is dependent on the size of the plant. The smallest councils are in firms with twenty-five employees, though there are some industries which are exempt such as railways and mining, ocean shipping and building. Surveys carried out in the 1960s showed that some 95 per cent of the larger plants with over 500 employees had a works council, while there were councils covering 80 per cent of the workers in other plants. Yet many workers thought that works councils had not been very effective.

Denmark

The Danes, like the Norwegians, have a relatively stable society with a homogeneous workforce. The rights of workers to organise were conceded around 1900. The Danish system developed on the same lines as the Norwegian, with agreements to negotiate and discuss where possible instead of striking.

Industrial councils were developed in the 1920s and a voluntary agreement on 'co-operative workshop councils' was reached on the iron and steel industry in 1926. Voluntary agreements on such councils were reached in 1947, their functions being seen as broadly consultative and designed to improve relations between workers and management. The councils, or committees, must receive the same information about the firm as do the shareholders.

In the years following 1945 an information drive, with speeches and pamphlets, helped to put across the role of works councils. Conferences were held and a network of supporters for the participative role of workers was created. The extension of works councils was to be based on voluntary negotiations and only secondly by legislative method.

Pressures developed in the late 1960s for an extension of industrial democracy and the Danish Federation of Trade Unions issued a report on democracy in industry.

By late 1964, the Danish Federation of Trade Unions and the Danish Employers' Confederation had joined together and produced an Agreement on Joint Consultation Committees (JCC), signed in October. The text of the Agreement states that a JCC shall be established in enterprises of fifty or more adult employees when 'either the employer or a majority of the workers propose it'. If this is not considered suitable, then the firm should hold unofficial meetings from time to time. The objectives of the JCC shall be to discuss and promote efficiency, changes and forms of rationalisation, vocational training, safety, welfare, etc. Information should be available to employees. The committees can also discuss incentive wage systems. The functions of the trade union are retained, as the committees cannot deal with matters relating to 'contractual or local wage agreements, which are normally determined by negotiation or arbitration' ('Agreement on Joint Consultation Committees', Copenhagen, 24 October 1964).

Surveys in Denmark showed that some 600 joint works councils existed by 1968 and fifty more by 1970. This accounted for 80 per cent of industry and trade. About 60 per cent of the councils have four meetings or more every year. The subjects discussed most were the state of the firm and employment, the manufacturing process, efficiency and personnel. Safety and welfare discussions were less frequent. Suggestion schemes grew rapidly, after initial sceptism, in the 1960s.

By 1971, the relative success of the joint committees had led the way for a development, on lines already followed in Norway, of co-operation committees. These are headed by a National Co-operative Council, consisting of three representatives each from unions and employers. There is a secretariat which gives guidance and directs research.

The Agreement on Co-operation and Co-operation Committees (Copenhagen, 2 October 1970) states its aims as 'day-to-day co-operation in all enterprises' with delegation of responsibility and more job satisfaction where possible. Workers are to have a share in decision-making. Rules are laid down for the setting-up, membership and functions of the co-operation committees. Emphasis is put on gaining the participation of all employees.

Norway

Works councils in Norway, as in Britain, stem from the aftermath of World War I, but in neither country did they survive in any large number. A revival took place in 1945 with joint production committees (JPC), but although there were 657 committees in 1961, their standing was not high. Yet they pointed the way to later developments in participation.

The agreement which set up the JPCs said that the aim was to promote the general well-being through co-operation and solidarity in industry, and utilise the experience and insight of the employees in order to increase efficiency, reduce costs and improve the competitive capacity of industry; for the benefit of the establishment, its employees must set up a JPC. Smaller plants need not, but often do so.

The results of the committees have varied from plant to plant, working most effectively in the larger plants. Some employers have been reluctant to discuss industrial methods with their employees, and vice versa, but attitudes have gradually changed as the two groups sat together and discussed industrial conditions freely and openly. This process has had far-reaching effects on collective bargaining, quite apart from the beneficial effect on productivity.

From the foundation and experience of the JPCs the Norwegian trade unions and the government have moved further into the area of industrial democracy, taking the view that capital is a social concept, managed by the owner subject to the consent of society. The labour movement holds that democracy means industrial as well as political democracy, and workers should be seen as partakers in the organisation of economic life.

Managers accept much of this point of view, except when it may directly conflict with the principle of economic efficiency. But the liberal social outlook in Norway has made for considerable rapport between management and unions on the issue of industrial democracy.

In the 1960s the labour government and employers and unions had a fresh look at the concept of workers' participation. One result of this was the abolition of the agreement about production committees. In its place the Co-operation Agreement was incorporated into the Basic Agreement.

The co-operation council The revised Co-operation Agreement carried forward the previous decisions about Production Committees, but the words 'production committee' are replaced by 'works councils'. These should be established in all companies with more than 100 employees.

Meetings of works councils are held monthly and the posts of chairman and vice-chairman are filled alternately by workers and employers. The information given the members is more complete than is the case in Britain, although the British Code of Industrial Relations (stemming from the 1971 Act) provides for members receiving the same kind of information as do shareholders. Information given to the Norwegian works councils deals with the economics of the firm and possible changes in technology and production. Other matters relate to welfare, safety and health, which most joint committees already discuss in most west European countries.

The Basic Agreement of 1966 also set up a completely new body, the Co-operation Council, in mid-1966. This consists of six members, three appointed by the trade union and three by the employers' confederation. The council has its own secretariat. The posts of chairman and vice-chairman are alternately taken by the managing director of the employers' confederation and the head of the trade union group. Each post is filled for a term of one year.

Functions of the council These can be divided into three main areas; information, training, and research. Information consists of providing information to and between the works council. Experience gained by one works council which is thought to be of general interest or use is also collected and circulated to other works councils.

The council also works in the field of training, as this is considered essential for the development of co-operation between employers and workers. This training usually takes place through established training centres and organisations.

In the field of research, the aim is to look at possible developments in the future which would aid the growth of co-operation in industry. Social scientists and other researchers are encouraged to give information about relevant research, which is then distributed.

The relationship between the council and its secretariat is that the cases are prepared and then considered by the council. The resolutions of the council which require action are carried out by the secretariat. When necessary, the council will appoint a committee to consider a special question or case. The field of research has a permanent working committee, called the Research Committee, with three representatives each from the trade union and the employers' confederation. The head of the secretariat acts as secretary to this committee.

Among the pamphlets circulated by the council were the shortest working week, the organisation and success of suggestion schemes, statistics on the establishment and activities of works councils. Since 1968 the council has arranged a number of one-day conferences for works councils in the different districts. These have been well attended, showing the interest which unions and management have in the subject.

Training and research activities It is one of the principles of the council that works council and department councils function most effectively if members have insight and knowledge about the problems on issues discussed. Companies are urged to arrange courses and conferences where the companies' activities can be explained and discussed. The secretariat of the council assists in the planning of such courses. As smaller companies usually find it more difficult to organise courses, joint courses are arranged for the committee members of such companies, and arranged according to requirements.

For general circulation, the council has prepared a correspondence course on the Norwegian economy and business. This is published under the title, *The Annual Report*. The course is designed to allow for local adaptations into the company's own training programme.

The council has been active in promoting research. The work has been planned in two phases, A and B. Phase A, 1960–4, resulted in the publication of *Industrial Democracy – Representation on the Company Board* (Universitetsforlaget, Oslo, 1964), and some arrangements for employee representatives on company boards. Phase B was concerned with the so-called field experiments, which are intended to do research in certain forms, with the approval of the main organisation, and the results of the experiments are then carried forward and tried out in new companies which have agreed to this being done. Phase B (1964–9) was designed to look at the field experiments on how to improve the conditions of employees' participation at work. Phase C (1970) envisages further experiments based on the researchers' findings.

Future developments

Though there is a well established system of workers' representation in western Europe, the trade unions have been pressing for changes to make this more effective and more democratic. Recent changes in Germany have given the works councils greater powers.

The Commission in Brussels made proposals in July 1971 for a European Company Statute. This would stipulate that workers would have at least one-third representation on the supervisory board. Further proposals have suggested a European Works Council for each European company drawn from workers in firms in the different countries. This will give impetus to the development of multi-national bargaining as well as to the spread of works councils in countries such as Britain.

⑨ Labour mobility, retraining and the European Social Fund

The Treaty of Rome states that there should be no barriers to the mobility of labour. This is the classic economic doctrine, which has seldom been seen in full operation for the past fifty years. Until the early 1920s, millions of people migrated from Europe to the USA, and this massive inflow of labour contributed to the rapid economic growth of that country.

Beginning in the 1920s and 1930s, countries in the western world withdrew into economic nationalisation and erected barriers against immigration, and in eastern Europe, against emigration. Since 1945, there have been movements of refugees across the face of Europe, moving west. Germany received a large inflow of *volksdeutsche* from East Germany and other areas, some seven million, and later three million from East Germany. From 1949 to 1959 the active labour force of Germany, Italy and the Netherlands rose by a compound annual percentage of 1·6, 1·1 and 1·5 respectively, although in the case of Italy the rise in the labour force was caused more by the movement of labour from the agricultural south, from heavy unemployment, to the industrial north, than to immigration.

In the 1960s, Germany and France, but especially the former, were absorbing large numbers of foreign workers as the national income and economy expanded. Large numbers of Italians went to Germany, as did Spaniards, Turks, Greeks and Yugoslavs. France absorbed about one million foreign workers, while some 40 per cent of the Swiss labour force was made up of foreign workers, which has caused problems of assimilation there.

These large-scale movements took place before, during and after the formulation of the Common Market, although more rapid economic growth lowered the level of unemployment and created an insatiable demand for workers (in June 1971, there were 900,000 unemployed in the UK, while West Germany had 750,000 job vacancies).

Rules on labour movement in the EEC

Full mobility of labour is officially allowed since 1968 and workers can move freely with either a passport or an identity card. They are given temporary residence permits for up to five years, thereafter renewable. If a worker has been unemployed for twelve months then his permit will only be renewed for another twelve months. A foreign worker can still be deported or prevented entry for various official reasons, for criminal, health, or other reasons.

Countries such as France and Netherlands, with former colonial territories, admit people from these territories to work. Such immigrants are not allowed free movement inside the EEC.

When Britain is a member of the EEC, this will pose for the first time the possibility of substantial numbers of coloured labour moving into the EEC. The crucial point is the UK government attitude to British nationality. Would the Kenyan Asians, holding British passports, be treated as 'nationals' by the EEC? Whatever the terms of the Rome Treaty on the free movement of labour, it does not seem that western Europe has any intention of allowing large-scale coloured immigration from the former British Commonwealth.

The EEC also stipulates that there is equality in employment opportunities between workers of different nationalities. All jobs are open, where vacancies occur, with the exception of public service at the higher levels. Migrant workers can bring their families with them, the term 'family' including a number of relatives from children to grandparents.

In practice, the majority of migrant workers in the EEC, notably the *Gastarbeiter* in Germany, are youngish men who come without their families, live in cramped quarters in bunk beds, spend little on rent and send a large part of their earnings back to their native country.

Large-scale mobility of labour took place before the freeing of all restrictions. The earlier stage was that workers could move to another country if no native worker had been found for the vacancy after a three-week period; his work permit was renewed after one year, and his family were allowed to come when adequate housing was available.

Effects of the EEC on labour mobility

It would seem that the movement of labour both inside and from outside the Common Market has been due more to the 'pull' of employment and the 'push' of unemployment than to the removal of barriers to mobility. Since 1960, the rate of unemployment in Germany has been under 1·0 per cent, and with the Berlin wall halting the flow of refugees from the east, workers migrated from Italy, which had one million unemployed, to the prosperous economy of Germany.

The Italian influx into Germany rose to its peak in 1960 with 73,000 workers, which declined to an outflow of 10,000 by 1964. The Italians arrived in the 1950s and 1960s with an employment permit or the work card of the ECSC. In 1962, for example, there were some 8,000 workers employed by the Federal Railways, of whom 6,500 were Italians. This is indicative of the harder and dirtier jobs undertaken by the migrant workers, as they were cleaning rolling stock and other unskilled work. As in other western countries with expanding economies and labour shortages, immigrant labour fills the vacancies in the mines, steelworks, construction, public transport industries, catering and textiles.

In the mid- and late-1960s the pattern of mobility inside the member countries of the EEC changed from the flow of unskilled and semi-skilled, to one of skilled technicians and experts. The sociological results of this shift in the quality of immigrant labour, accompanied by families, led to greater integration and acceptance within the host country. Previously, and to some extent still, migrant workers had been younger men, or men who left wives and families behind. They tended, because of language difficulties, to live in crowded compounds or hostels in which they could live cheaply and send money back home. This sometimes led to tension with the nationals of the country employing them, e.g. France with Algerians, Germany with Turks and other south European *gastarbeiter*.

Wider labour markets

One labour market in which there has been free movement of

workers is that of the steel and coal industries of the Six. In reality, there has been little inter-community movement, as the official labour cards for trans-national movement are only issued to skilled workers and these barely reach 2,000. This rule means little in itself, as numbers of workers move without such cards. Another, and more important, reason for the lack of inter-Community mobility, is that there has been keen demand for skilled workers so that few felt the need to move to another country.

The effect of these factors is that a big inflow of unskilled labour has come from Italy, Greece, Turkey and Spain, so that the effect of the ECSC has done little to stimulate the movement of workers between the coal and steel areas of the EEC. Yet this is not in itself a test of Community labour policy as miners in areas where mines are being closed tend to be older and less mobile than workers in more modern industries. The same applies, in a lesser sense, to redundant steel workers.

The same lack of mobility has been noticed in another inter-country labour market, that formed by the Benelux countries. The net movement of workers has been relatively small, though this is not surprising as the demand for labour came from the Belgian coal mines, to which, as the above comment showed, few miners will move and the vacant places are filled by Italians, Slavs and Turks.

Common employment has existed between the Scandinavian countries since 1954. The movement of labour has not been great. This is understandable, as employment has been high in these countries, and unemployed men can usually find jobs near their home.

The Common Market has created more job opportunities, but does not seem to have led to greater mobility of labour between member countries. This is hardly surprising when we consider that most of the Six have a high level of employment. It is the high employment levels and the demand for labour which appears to have led to worker immigration, and not mainly the Community policy on labour. This has acted as a regulatory device between high employment countries and those with high unemployment. As most of these, with the exception of southern Italy, lie outside the Common Market area, e.g. Spain, Turkey, Greece, this explains the relatively low mobility of the west European workers (on this theme, see G. Reid and L. Hunter, 'Integration and Labour

Mobility', in *International Labor*, S. Barkin (ed.), Harper & Row, N.Y. and London, 1967).

An illustration of the way in which high unemployment levels act as a 'push' factor towards high employment areas, even with the barriers of distance and language, can be seen from the estimate that the present number of British citizens working in Germany (17,000) will rise to 150,000 by 1980. As the British had over 900,000 unemployed in September 1971, while the Germans had some 750,000 job vacancies, it seems that this estimate is not exaggerated. In view of the language difficulties, the mobile workers are likely to be the young workers, perhaps some of those who served recently in the forces in Germany, and some of the younger professional men.

The EEC and manpower policy

There are a number of specific statements in the Treaty of Rome which refer to the need for a rising standard of living based on a high level of employment. Unemployment is to be kept to a minimum, redundancy payments are to be closely linked to earning power and retraining and resettlement grants are to be generous and widely used.

Article 1 says that members' aims are 'constantly improving the living and working conditions of their peoples'; Article 3 of the European Social Fund set up 'to improve the possibilities of employment for workers' and their standard of living. Articles 39, 48, 49, deal with the full use of labour, the free movement of workers, and the collaboration of countries to achieve 'free choice of employment', setting up machinery for matching the demand for and the supply of labour, and thus avoiding lower living standards and employment in some regions.

Other Articles refer to the high employment and living standards, aims to which member countries pledge themselves. These are the group of Articles which refer to the social conditions of the Treaty of Rome (J. Dedieu, 'The European Economic Community', in 'International Trade Union Seminar on Active Manpower Policy' (mimeographed report), OECD, Vienna, September 1963, pp. 93-109).

While regional policies are a feature of all the countries of the Common Market, some could run into difficulties on a strict interpretation of the Treaty of Rome which opposes subsidies to help exports, which the British REP might do. But it seems that government help for firms to set up in the high unemployment areas of the member country would be permitted. Several countries also pursue policies of influencing industrial location, e.g. the French try to direct new industrial development away from the major industrial area around Paris towards the south-west, Holland and Belgium have regional policies which have set up development areas and subsidise firms. Even Germany, with its belief in a free 'social economy' has a number of redevelopment areas and loans to firms.

Italy has probably the greatest regional problem of the Six. For many years the South has been the low growth, rural and over-populated area with high unemployment. Income per head in most of the South is about half that of the national average. A development bank was set up, the *Cassa per il Mezzogiorno,* to assist and develop industry and agriculture in the South by large investments. There is a widespread system of loans and subsidies.

These regional policies in the Six have helped the movement of labour and the creating of jobs in the more depressed areas. While this has helped, the Birkelbach Report (1963) stated that the beneficial effects had been more due to the movement of labour out of the depressed areas, than to the creation of new jobs in these areas.

Early in 1972, M. Albert Coppé, Commissioner for Social Policy of the EEC, reported that the regional problem, higher unemployment in the peripheral regions, still existed. Not enough was being spent on the retraining of workers in declining areas. He urged the member countries to look again at this problem, as the unemployment figures in the Six, and especially in Italy, were rising.

Government training for the jobless is more advanced in France and Germany than it is in Britain, where the jobless total is much larger. France has 120 centres under the *l'Association Nationale pour la Formation Professionelle des Adultes,* run jointly by the Ministry of Labour, employers' associations and trade unions. A wide range of training is provided, and 50,000 were trained in 1970, in a labour force of 20·5 million. This compares with a figure of 18,400 in Britain in a labour force of 25 million. France has also a Collective Agreement (July 1970), covering half the labour force, which allows workers to retrain without loss of earnings or losing their jobs.

Germany supports training programmes through the Federal Institute of Labour, which is financed by the Social Insurance Fund. 190,000 workers (labour force 26 million) received money from the Institute. Employees can have time off from work to attend courses. If one-third of his working time is spent on a course, the worker is eligible for an allowance 'in lieu of wages'.

Britain has undoubtedly been influenced in its attitude to job training by the European schemes, as well as by its highest unemployment figures, over one million in early 1972, for over thirty years. In February 1972, the British government announced a great expansion of job training, from a figure of under 20,000 yearly to one of 100,000 a year. This was to be in stages, with the target for 1957 being 60,000-70,000. This was to be achieved by the phasing out of the Industrial Training Board (ITB) levy-grant system, and the setting up of an independent national training agency which would co-ordinate the future and different functions of the ITB, and be responsible to the Secretary of State for Employment for all training activities (the information on training is drawn from *Training for the Future*, Department of Employment, HMSO, London, 1972).

The European Social Fund

The Social Fund was set up under the Treaty of Rome with the aim of raising living standards by assisting workers to move freely between countries and occupations (Articles 125-8). At the request of member countries the Fund provides up to 50 per cent of the costs of retraining or resettling labour, and makes payments towards those who have been made redundant. In effect, the Fund attempts to cushion the effects of economic change, and is intended to be of most use in the areas of high unemployment. The Fund can also carry out studies of problems and social questions.

The Social Fund has drawn on the experience of the European Coal and Steel Community which had a similar fund for retraining and redundancy necessary in the basic industries, especially mining, where large-scale redundancies were anticipated. The ECSC scheme paid workers who were waiting for new jobs, and differential allowances between their previous wages and those received in their new job, a payment which could last for two years. The ECSC fund paid 50 per cent of the cost of these social payments and the respective countries paid the other half. Between 1954 and 1970, 429,000 workers in coal and steel received $300 million in help to find new employment. Finance has also been available for the housing of coal and steel workers.

The member states of the Community pay a fixed scale of contributions into the Fund, with the larger and wealthier countries paying more (France and Germany 32 per cent, Italy 20 per cent and Belgium 8·8 per cent as against the Netherlands 7 per cent). Italy pays rather less than its size would warrant, and one of the main effects of the Social Fund has been to help the regional policy and high unemployment difficulties of the country.

In 1971 it was decided to widen the area of the Fund and two new types of intervention were introduced (1) to help those whose jobs were affected by rationalisation and needed assistance, (2) retraining and resettlement for those workers who are already unemployed. On the urging of the Italian government, much of the new types of assistance from the Social Fund has gone to help in the poorer areas of Italy, particularly the South.

The EEC is linking the Fund to its manpower surveys. These show that the long-term movement of labour from agriculture to industry and the cities will continue. One estimate is that in the ten years 1970–80 some two million farmers will have to find work outside agriculture. From 1970–5 it is forecast there will be between 200,000 and 400,000 workers leaving textiles through redundancies, while 200,000 miners will leave the coal industry (the last-named are assisted by the ECSC). Other industries will be going through structural and technological changes and one worker in ten could change his job in ten years due to these shifts in the economy (*European Community*, August/September 1970, p. 7).

One of the changes in Fund policy will be that private bodies will now be assisted, in addition to the public organisations which had previously benefited. Wider definitions will be given to the term 'worker' so that migrant labour from outside the EEC may also be eligible. A Community social budget has been proposed, which would collect statistics on social security and social policy. Plans were to be made from the data collected, and estimates made as to the effects of harmonisation of social policies on the various member states.

1⓪ Systems of social security

The system of social security in a country interacts with industrial relations in that it provides a backing to wages, pensions, sickness, injury benefits and other payments or benefits provided by the firm. Systems differ, with the British system, based on the Beveridge Plan, providing a flat-rate payment for claimants (later extended to earnings-related benefits) administered by the State, to that of the USA, where the State has played a minimal role and the unions and employers have built up a considerable system of plant and union related insurance.

The west European systems, some of which pre-dated the British national insurance system, are based primarily on the State, but the administration and incidence varies between countries. The Treaty of Rome emphasis on the harmonisation of taxation and benefits must bring forth some interesting comparisons between its member states. In addition to the present differences between countries, the Common Market for labour will pose problems of social insurance for the mobile workers. Conceivably, some could be in several countries for short periods (building construction, technologists), though more probably the mobile worker will be in a country where he pays insurance and sends part of his wage back to his home country, e.g. the Italians.

The EEC considered the question of social security and produced the European Agreement on Social Security (Regulation No. 3 of the EEC). The rule said that a worker's social security is based on his place of work. If he is sent to another country to work by the employer, then his social insurance is paid at or from his place of employment. If employed in the other country, he comes under the social security acts there (A. Kayser, in Barkin (ed.), op. cit.). In some cases the workers have a plurality of systems and make the choice between them. (Articles 117-18 of the Treaty of Rome call for harmonisation of social security 'with a view to overall social improvement'.)

The effects of the Common Market have had some effect on social security in France. This is a country where unemployment insurance has been partly due to collective bargaining by the unions, with a general system covering workers in commerce and industry being negotiated in 1958. One reason given for the lack of unemployment insurance is said to be that unemployment has never risen to the levels of more industrialised western countries. One US expert on French industrial relations writes, noting the need for reciprocity in social benefits in the Six, 'But France and Italy had no comprehensive system of unemployment insurance, and consequently little to offer in the way of reciprocal benefits' (F. Meyers, 'The Role of Collective Bargaining in France', *B.J.I.R.*, Vol. III, No. 3, 1965).

A German government publication states that the aim of the social security system is to be based on individual responsibility 'if a person capable of work has fallen in want through no fault of his own he is to be assisted generously. At the same time there can be no question of introducing a system of allowances which would lead to the creation of an egalitarian Welfare State' (*Germany Reports*, Federal German Embassy, London, 1964, p. 18). In spite of this assertion, the German worker has an earnings-related pension when he retires, which is considerably higher (over three times) than was the case in Britain in 1971. To finance his social security benefits, the German workers' weekly contribution is over twice what it is in Britain. This in itself helps to keep down the pace of inflation, by taking present spending power out of circulation for future consumption.

The State and social security benefits

Over ten years ago, when the Common Market countries were poorer, they still paid higher social security benefits in most cases than did the British. If we take the case of a steelworker, who is married with two children, we find (Table 5) that he received monthly payment in different countries (as a percentage of his monthly wages) in 1959, for the various reasons indicated.

Table 5 *Compensation as a percentage of wages*

Country	Sickness	Industrial injury or disease/ temporary 100% disablement	Family allowance	Unemployment
France	39	47	19	40
Germany	71	71	2	52
Italy	48	68	17	19
Belgium	67	71	12	42
Holland	76	76	7	80
Luxembourg	55	78	11	56
UK	34	46	3	32

If we compare these percentages with Britain in 1959, we find that Britain lags well behind in social security benefits, especially in those connected with industrial work, or lack of it. When Mr Macmillan borrowed an Americanism in 1959 and told the British 'You have never had it so good' he could not have been referring to statutory social security.

Britain showed up better in the 1950s in the payment of non-statutory payments provided by firms to their employees, especially for old age or invalidity, employment injury and sickness. (I.L.R. 1958.)

Yet, at the same time, comparisons of the systems of social security in Britain and the Common Market countries is fraught with difficulties. One joint study between the EEC and the National Coal Board spoke of the absence or scarceness of information on numerous points, and of the complexity and diversity of social security systems, not only between Britain and the EEC countries, but also between the countries of the Community (E.E.C., 'Rapport sur la comparaison du Système Britannique de Securité Sociale avec les Systèmes des Pays de la Communauté, 1968).

The EEC Report mentions, however, a fundamental difference of principle between the social security of Britain and of the EEC countries. In general, the British system provides for a social minimum. In contrast, the EEC countries are more selective, confining themselves more to those who have need of social security or provision. Payments or benefits for those at work tend to be related to earnings, which in turn means a different contribution related to income.

The differences between the two types of system, one general and providing a social minimum, the other selective and earnings-related, represents a basic difference in approach. The British scheme is, or was, egalitarian in its objective, as the system led to some transfer of income from the richer groups to the poorer ones, and to some narrowing of income differentials. The EEC system could lead to a widening of differentials and of income differences between social groups. Occupational pensions are more common in the EEC, although some types of insurance, e.g. old age pensions, are on a general scale, and there are recent signs that some countries are introducing more general coverage. Britain has also moved in recent years towards earnings-related benefits and supplementary benefits to the social minimum related to needs.

Other differences between Britain and the EEC are the variety of bodies dealing with social security in the EEC compared with the highly centralised system in Britain. Old age pensions are linked to the cost of living index in the EEC, which Britain is now preparing to follow.

Every country in the EEC spends more money per head of population on social welfare and security than does Britain and also a higher percentage of the GNP. Each of the Six spends between 15·9 per cent of GNP (France) and 17·5 per cent (Netherlands) compared with 12·4 per cent for Britain.

Table 6   *Percentages paid of total social security payment*

	Employer	Employee	State
France	69	22	9
Germany	49	31	20
Italy	66	17	17
Belgium	50	23	27
Netherlands	46	39	15
UK	20	22	58

Another difference between Britain and the EEC is the method of financing social security, through which employers pay a large proportion compared with that of the employees and the State.

The figures in Table 6 illustrate the important differences in the methods of financing social security. These methods in turn affect the labour costs of the French and Italian employers, which raises the final price of the product. There are signs that the British government intends to shift the incidence of taxation from income tax on the individual to consumers' expenditure. This would be regressive or discriminatory against the poorer groups of the population, although it might provide a greater incentive for the higher paid. Britain is also moving towards higher social security benefits based on higher contributions.

The differences between Britain and the Six in financing social security lie in the proportion which comes from taxation as compared with contributions from employer and employee. In Britain, contributions account for 45 per cent, in the Six between 60 and 90 per cent of total cost. The rest comes from taxation.

Table 7   *Percentage of social security benefits to gross national product, 1965*

France	15·9
Germany	15·6
Italy	15·5
Belgium	14·5
Netherlands	15·4

A. Delperee, 'Social Security in the European Economic Community', *International Institute for Labour Studies, Bulletin No. 8*, 1971, p. 33. Britain spent some 3 per cent less in this period.

Harmonisation of social security benefits is assumed in Articles 117-18 of the Treaty of Rome. As we see from Table 7, France is spending the highest proportion of GNP on social security, and the employer, or his industrial costs, is bearing the majority part of the costs. We may assume that harmonisation will lead to a rise in the level of social security benefits to the level of the highest benefits being paid. For Britain this will mean a substantial increase in benefits and, under the present British system, a rise in general taxation or employees' contributions. The alternative is to follow the continental pattern and raise the relative contribution of the employer.

Table 8   *Paid holidays in the EEC*

Country	Minimum annual paid holiday (*in days*)	Public holidays	Total
France	24	9	33
Belgium	18 (a)	10	28
Germany	15-24 (b)	10-13	25-37
Italy	12-30	17	29-47
Netherlands	18-23 (a)	6- 7	24-30
Luxembourg	18-24	10	28-34
United Kingdom	generally 15	6	21

(a) Plus holiday bonus equal to 2 weeks pay.
(b) Plus bonuses.

Select bibliography

General

KASSALOW, E. M., *Trade Unions and Industrial Relations: An International Comparison*, Random House, N.Y., 1969. (Part One deals with western Europe, Part Two with the new nations.)
STURMTHAL, A., *Contemporary Collective Bargaining in Seven Countries*, Cornell University Press, N.Y., 1957.
STURMTHAL, A., *Workers' Councils*, Harvard University Press, Cambridge, Mass., 1964.

Countries

United Kingdom

CLEGG, H., *The System of Industrial Relations in Great Britain*, Blackwell, 1970.
HMSO, *Royal Commission on Trade Unions and Employers' Associations* (the Donovan Report), London, 1968.

France

DELAMOTTE, Y., 'Recent Collective Bargaining Trends in France', *Int. Lab. Rev.*, April 1971, pp. 247-68.
LORVIN, V., *The Labor Movement in France*, Harvard University Press, Cambridge, Mass., 1954.
OECD, *France: Economic Survey*, Paris, 1968.
OECD, *France: Economic Survey*, Paris, 1971.

Germany

EDELMAN, M. and FLEMING, R. W., *Politics of Wage–Price Decisions: A Four Country Analysis*, University of Illinois Press, Urbana, 1965.
MEYERS, F., *European Coal Mining Unions*, Institute of Industrial Relations, University of California, Los Angeles, 1961 (deals also with France, Belgium, and Great Britain).
OECD, *Germany: Economic Survey*, Paris, 1970.
OECD, *Germany: Economic Survey*, Paris, 1971.

Italy

GUIGNI, G., 'Recent Developments in Collective Bargaining in Italy', *Int. Lab. Rev.*, April 1965, pp. 273-91.

HOROWITZ, D., *The Italian Labor Movement*, Harvard University Press, Cambridge, Mass., 1964.

OECD, *Italy: Economic Survey*, Paris, 1971.

Belgium

BLANPAIN, R., 'Recent Trends in Collective Bargaining in Belgium', *Int. Lab. Rev.*, July-August 1971, pp. 111-29.

OECD, *Belgium–Luxembourg Economic Union: Economic Survey*, Paris, 1970.

SEYFORTH, SHAW, FAIRWEATHER and GERALDSON, *Labor Relations and the Law in Belgium and the United States*, Vol. 2, University of Michigan, Ann Arbor, 1970.

Netherlands

OECD, *Netherlands: Economic Survey*, Paris, 1970.

WINDMULLER, JOHN W., *The Labor Movement in the Netherlands*, Cornell University Press, N.Y., 1969.

Denmark

GALENSON, W. (ed.), *Comparative Labor Movements*, Harvard University Press, Cambridge, Mass., 1952 (see also for Norway).

OECD, *Denmark: Economic Survey*, Paris, 1970.

PEDERSON, J., 'Incomes Policy – Danish Style', *Banca Nazionale del Lavoro Quarterly Review*, No. 69, June 1964, pp. 160-82.

Norway

DORFMAN, H., *Labor Relations in Norway*, Oslo, 1966.

OECD, *Norway: Economic Survey*, Paris, 1971.

Ireland

BLUM, A. A., 'Strikes, Salaries and the Search for Solutions: An Interpretive Analysis of the Irish Industrial Relations System', *B.I.J.R.*, Vol. X, No. 1, March 1972, pp. 62-83.

BROWNE, M. H., 'Industrial Labour and Incomes Policy in the Republic of Ireland', *B.J.I.R.*, Vol. III, No. 1, March 1965, pp. 46-66.

OECD, *Ireland: Economic Survey*, Paris, 1971.